Origami Twelve Days of Christmas

And Santa, too!

Second Edition

Origami Twelve Days of Christmas

And Santa, too!

Second Edition

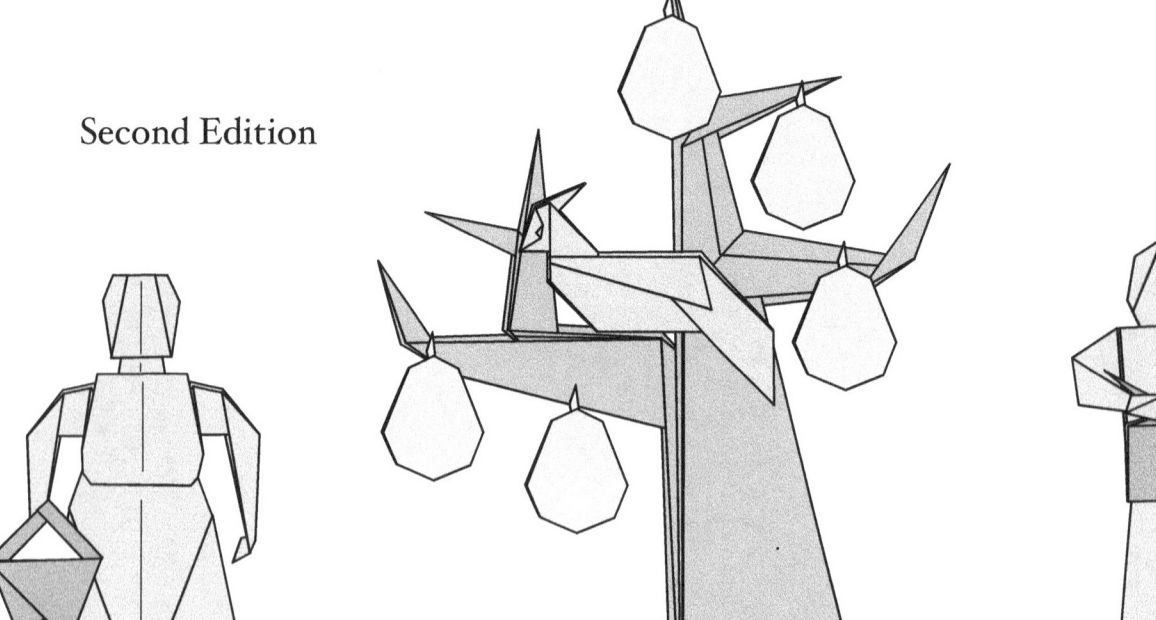

John Mon

Antroll Publishing Company

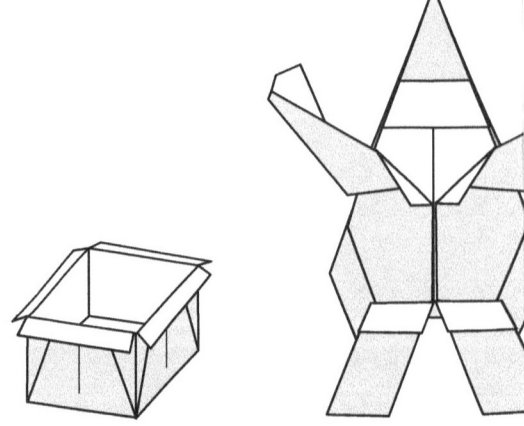

Introduction

Decorate the Christmas season with origami. You can fold scenes from the Twelve Days of Christmas and make models for the Christmas tree. There are 36 models from simple to intermediate. Most of the models are original and a few are traditional favorites.

With the Partridge, you can also fold a tree with pears to create a complete scene. The two Turtle Doves are shown with a heart. The Ladies and Lords bring more spirit as intermediate level models. Along with Santa Claus, there are toys, boxes, and tree ornaments. The ambitious folder can make Christmas cards by pasting the models on the cards to make familiar scenes.

The diagrams conform to the internationally approved Randlett-Yoshizawa style. Although any square paper can be used for the projects in this book, the best material is origami paper. The colored side of origami paper is represented by the shadings in the diagrams. Origami supplies are found at arts and crafts stores, or at Origami USA: www.origamiusa.org. Online sites such as OrigamiUSA will help you find local, national, and international groups practicing the art of origami around the world.

I thank Himanshu Agrawal for folding the cover models and taking the photos. For the new folder, I hope this is a fun introduction to origami.

John Montroll

www.johnmontroll.com

Contents

Symbols 9
Basic Folds 10
Twelve Days of Christmas 13
And Santa, too! 45

Partridge 14

Pear 16

Tree 17

Turtle Dove 19

Heart 21

French Hen 23

Calling Bird 25

Christmas Tree 27

Golden Ring 28

Goose 29

Swan 31

Sailboat 32

6 *Origami Twelve Days of Christmas*

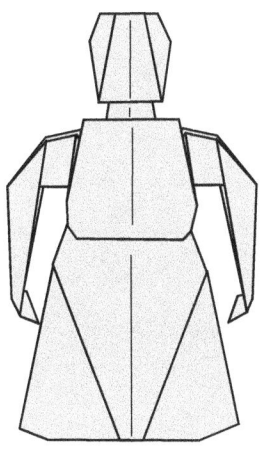
Maid a-Milking 33

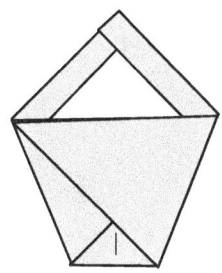
Pail 36

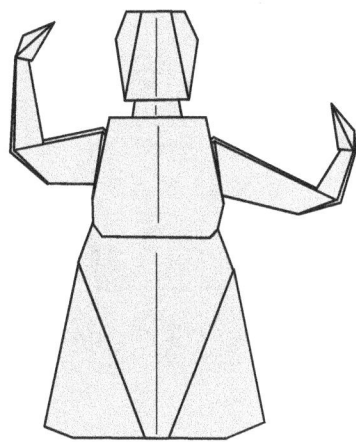
Lady Dancing 37

Lord a-Leaping 38

Piper Piping 41

Pipe 42

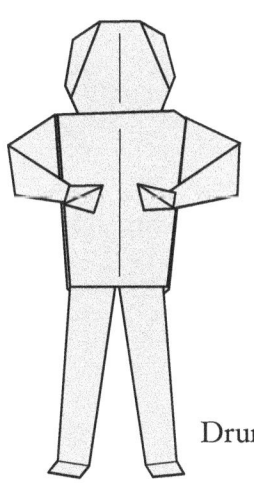
Drummer Drumming 43

Drum 44

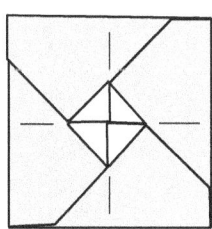
Fancy Card 46

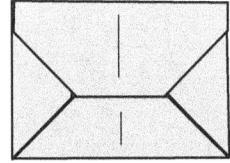
Envelope 47

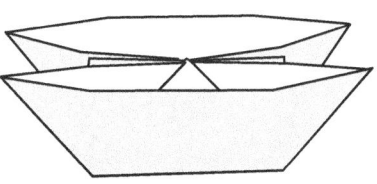
Catamaran 47

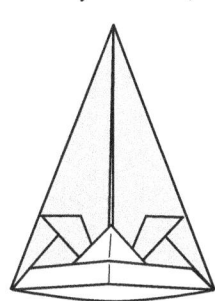
Party Hat 48

Contents 7

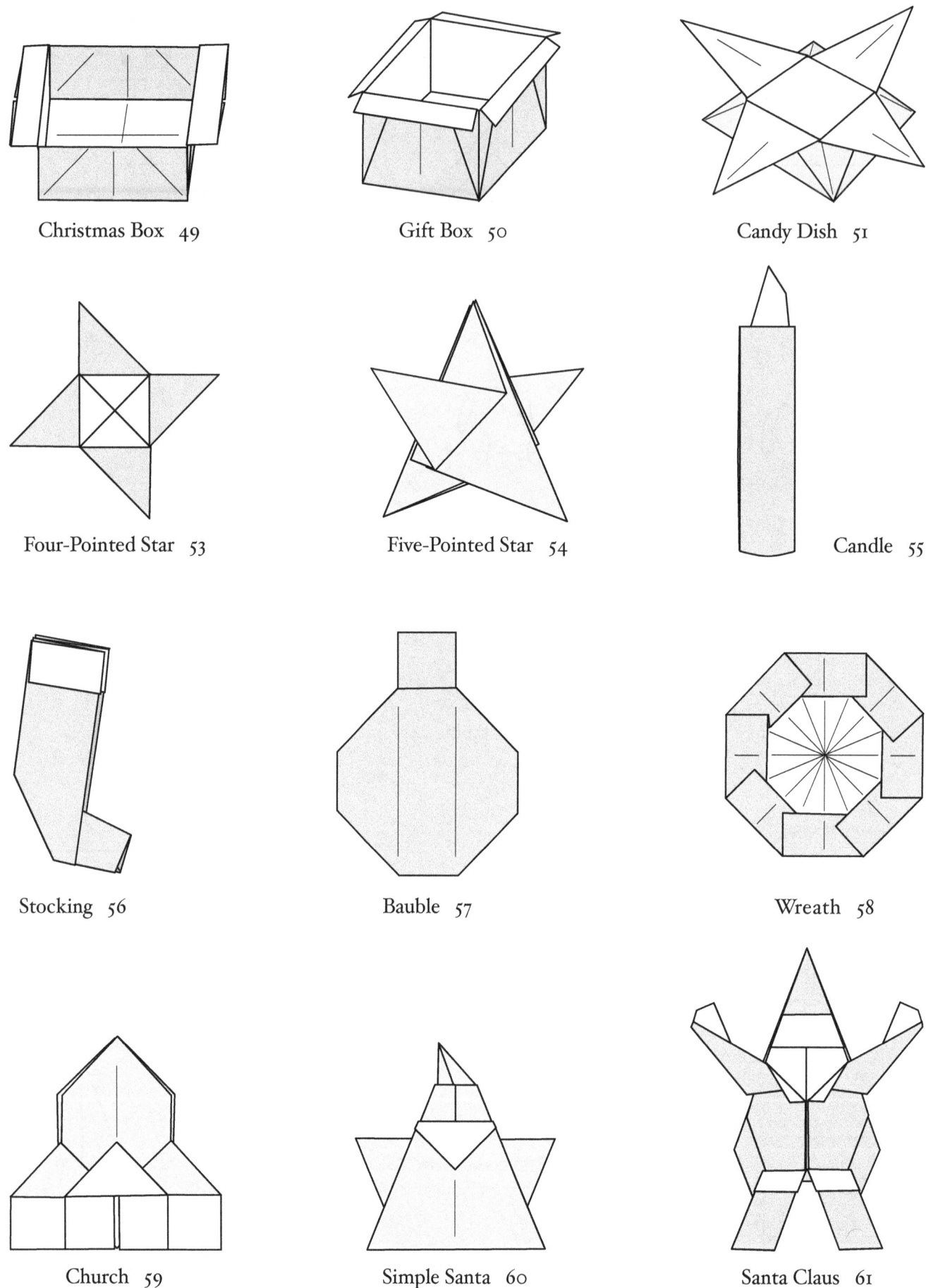

8 *Origami Twelve Days of Christmas*

Symbols

Lines

– – – – – – – – –   Valley fold, fold in front.

–··–··–··–··–··–   Mountain fold, fold behind.

————————   Crease line.

··················   X-ray or guide line.

Arrows

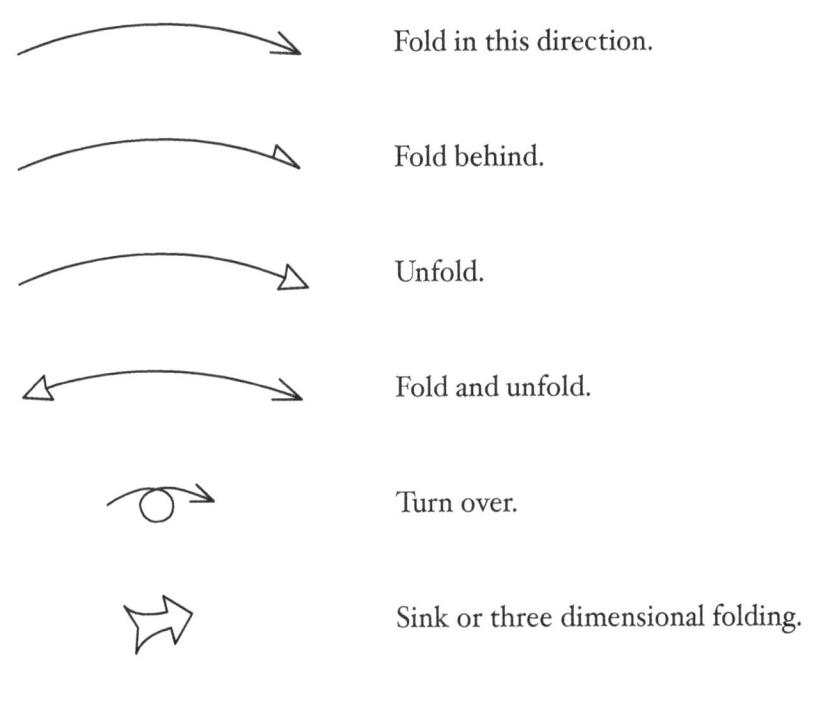

Fold in this direction.

Fold behind.

Unfold.

Fold and unfold.

Turn over.

Sink or three dimensional folding.

Place your finger between these layers.

Basic Folds

Pleat Fold.

Fold back and forth. Each pleat is composed of one valley and mountain fold. Here are two examples.

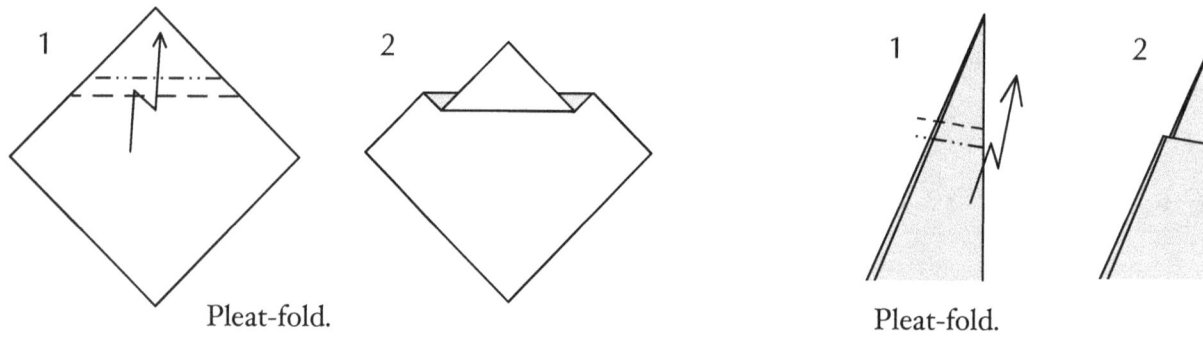

Squash Fold.

In a squash fold, some paper is opened and then made flat. The shaded arrow shows where to place your finger.

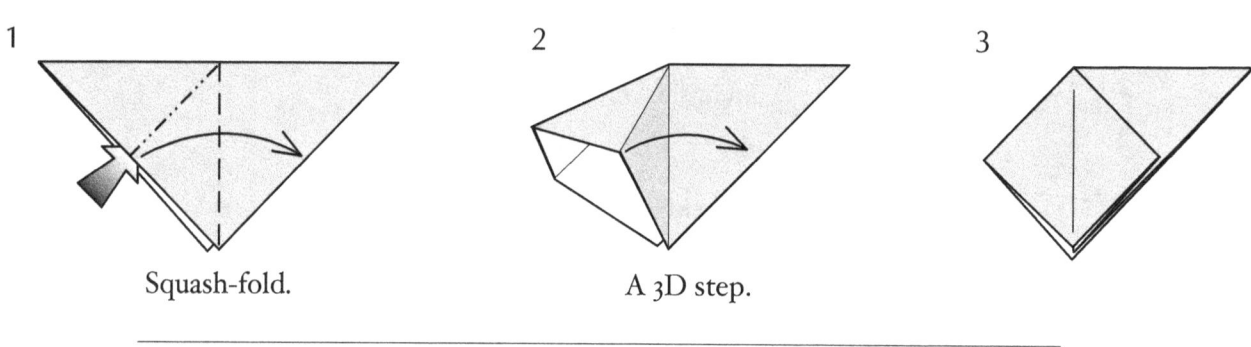

Petal Fold.

In a petal fold, one point is folded up while two opposite sides meet each other.

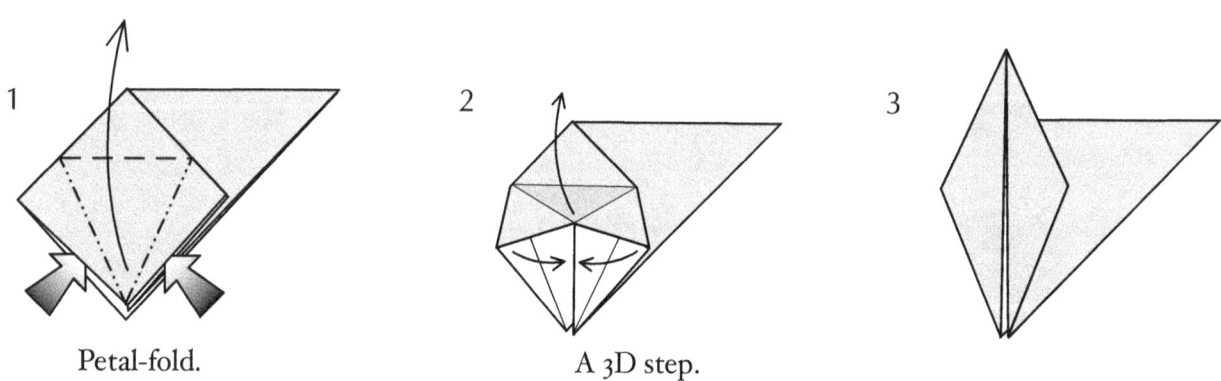

Inside Reverse Fold.

In an inside reverse fold, some paper is folded between layers. Here are two examples.

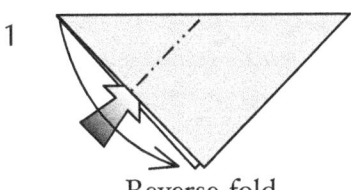
Reverse-fold.

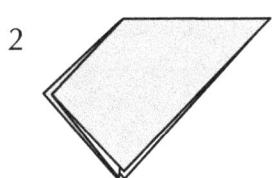

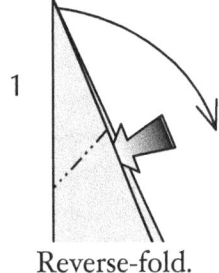
Reverse-fold.

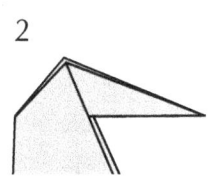

Outside Reverse Fold.

Much of the paper must be unfolded to make an outside reverse fold.

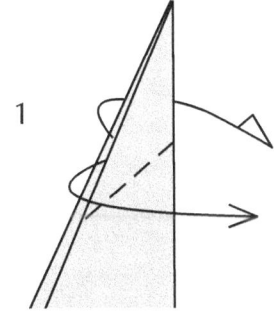
Outside-reverse-fold.

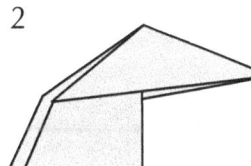

Crimp Fold.

A crimp fold is a combination of two reverse folds. Open the model slightly to form the crimp evenly on each side. Here are two examples.

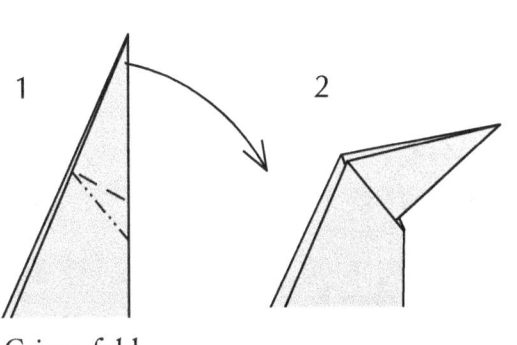
Crimp-fold.

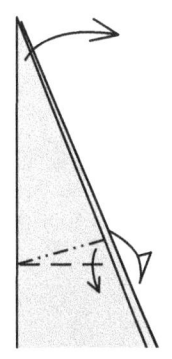
Crimp-fold.

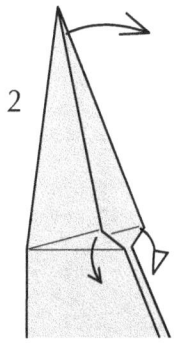
A 3D step.

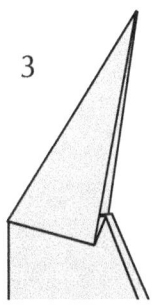

Basic Folds 11

Preliminary Fold.

The Preliminary Fold is the starting point for many models. The maneuver in step 3 occurs in many other models.

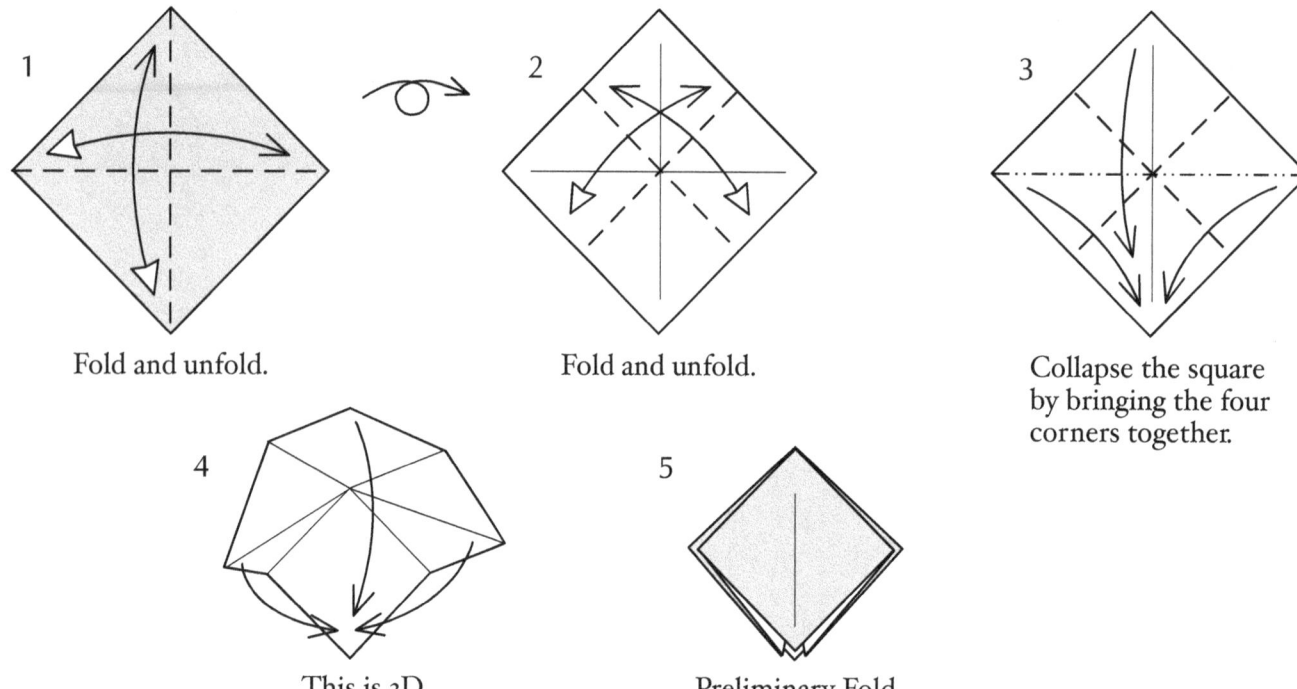

1. Fold and unfold.
2. Fold and unfold.
3. Collapse the square by bringing the four corners together.
4. This is 3D.
5. Preliminary Fold

Waterbomb Base.

The waterbomb base is named from the waterbomb balloon which is made from it.

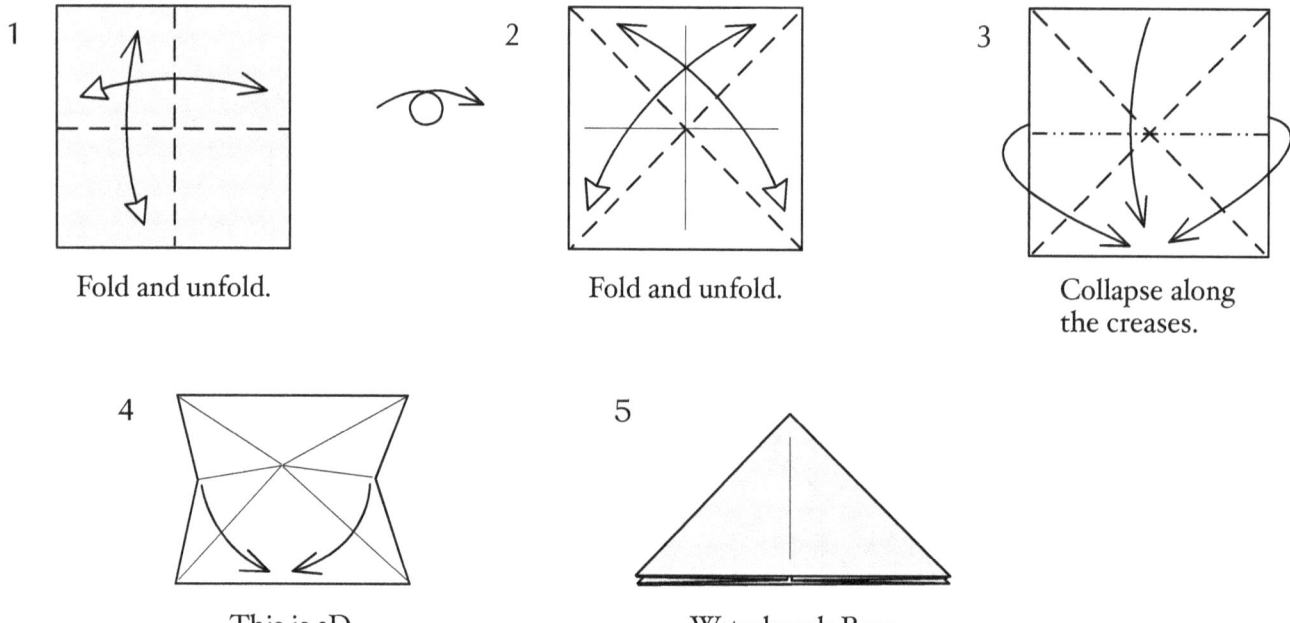

1. Fold and unfold.
2. Fold and unfold.
3. Collapse along the creases.
4. This is 3D.
5. Waterbomb Base

12 *Origami Twelve Days of Christmas*

Twelve Days of Christmas

On the twelfth day of Christmas,
  my true love sent to me

Twelve drummers drumming,

Eleven pipers piping,

Ten lords a-leaping,

Nine ladies dancing,

Eight maids a-milking,

Seven swans a-swimming,

Six geese a-laying,

Five golden rings,

Four calling birds,

Three French hens,

Two turtle doves,

And a partridge
in a pear tree.

Partridge

On the first day of Christmas,
my true love sent to me
A partridge in a pear tree.

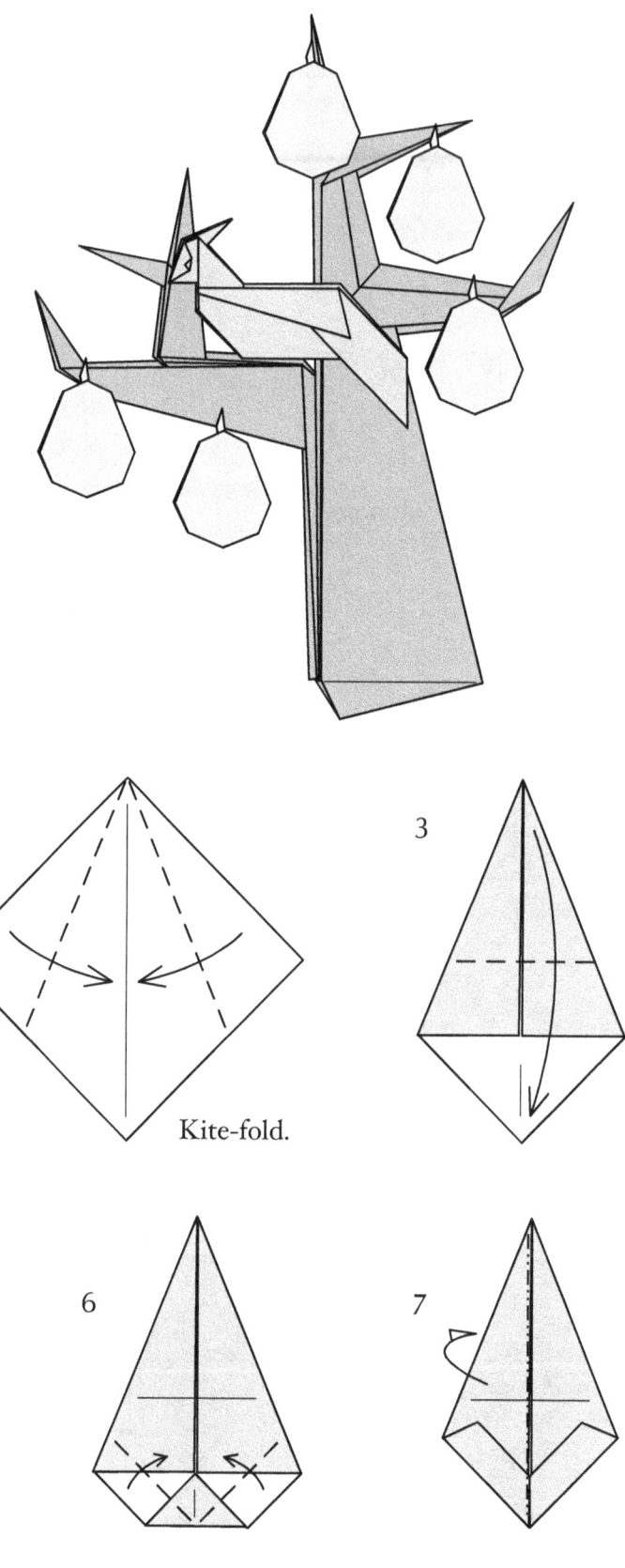

1. 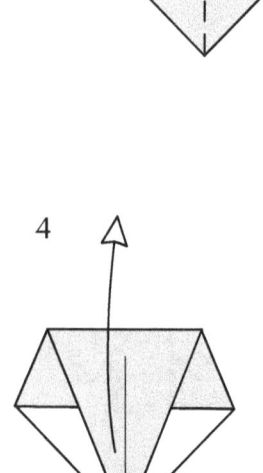 Fold and unfold.

2. Kite-fold.

3.

4. 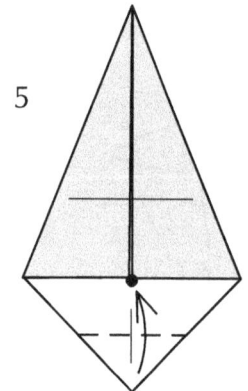 Unfold.

5.

6.

7. Fold in half and rotate.

14 *Origami Twelve Days of Christmas*

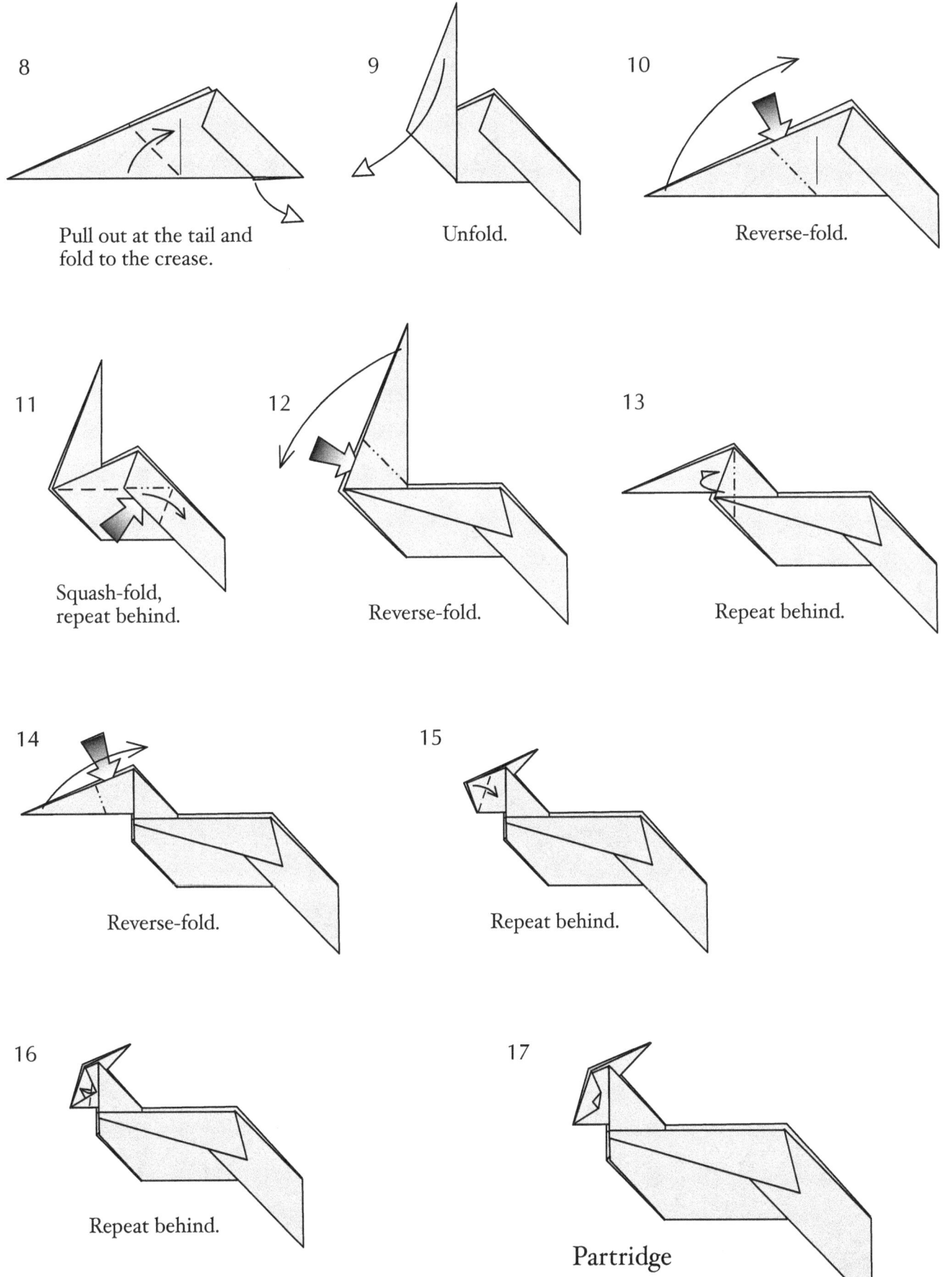

Partridge

Pear

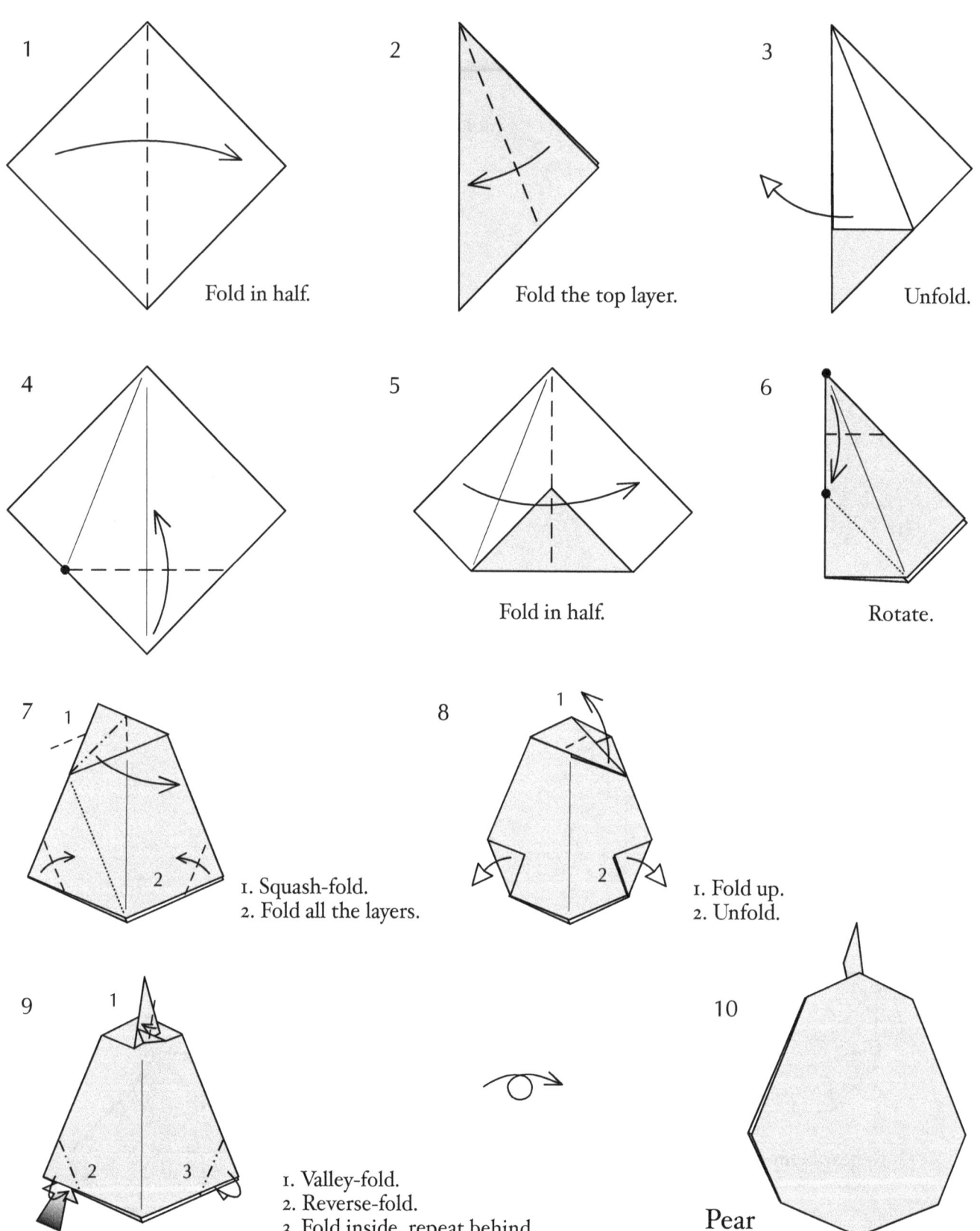

1. Fold in half.
2. Fold the top layer.
3. Unfold.
5. Fold in half.
6. Rotate.
7. 1. Squash-fold. 2. Fold all the layers.
8. 1. Fold up. 2. Unfold.
9. 1. Valley-fold. 2. Reverse-fold. 3. Fold inside, repeat behind.
10. Pear

16 *Origami Twelve Days of Christmas*

Tree

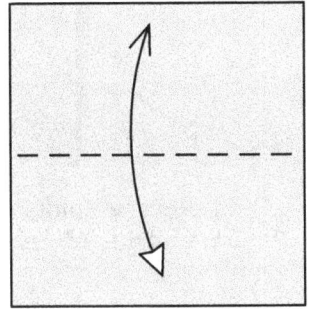

1. Fold and unfold.

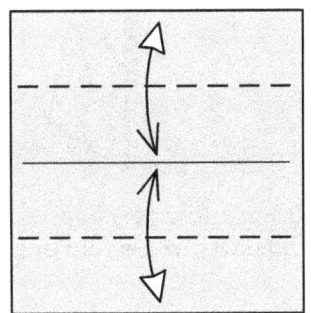

2. Fold and unfold.

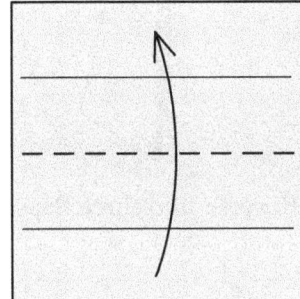

3.

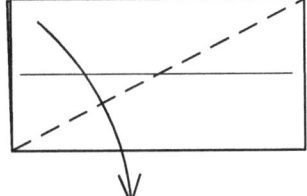

4. Fold the top layer. Repeat behind.

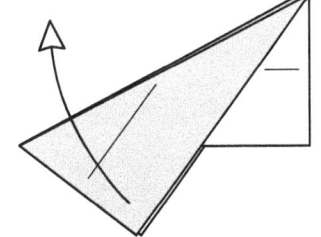

5. Unfold, repeat behind.

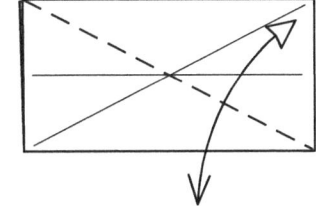

6. Fold and unfold. Repeat behind.

7

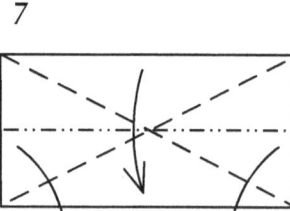

Fold along the creases.

8

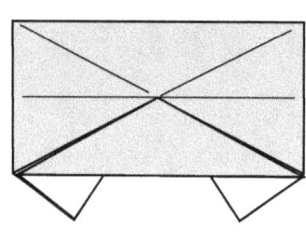

Repeat step 7 behind.

9

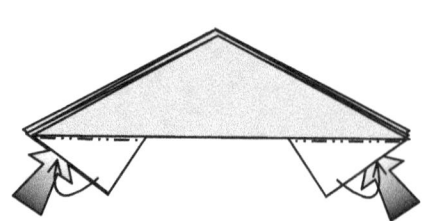

Reverse folds. Repeat behind.

10

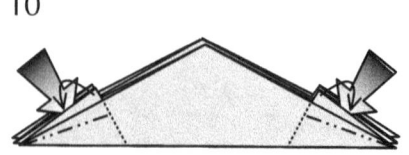

Reverse folds. Repeat behind.

11

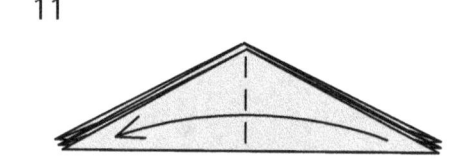

Fold in half and rotate.

12

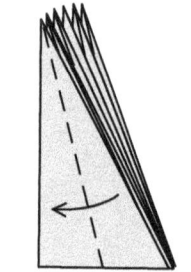

Fold all the layers.

13

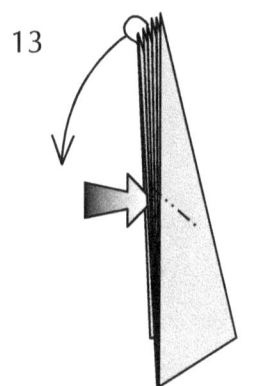

Reverse-fold three flaps.

14

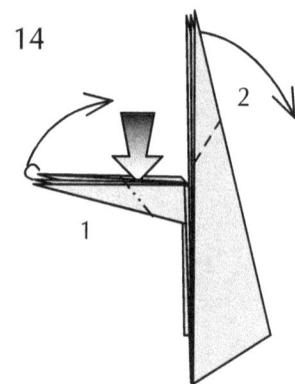

1. Reverse-fold two flaps.
2. Outside-reverse-fold one flap.

15

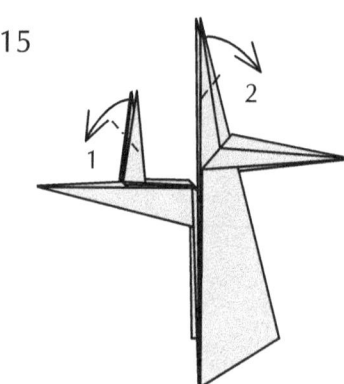

1. Reverse-fold.
2. Outside-reverse-fold.

16

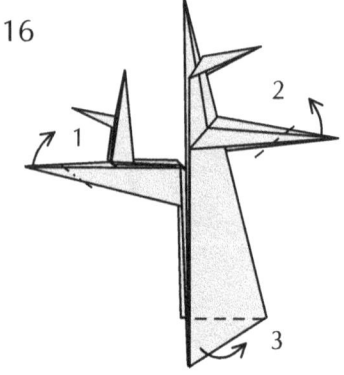

1. Reverse-fold.
2. Outside-reverse-fold.
3. Lift up slightly so the tree can stand.

17

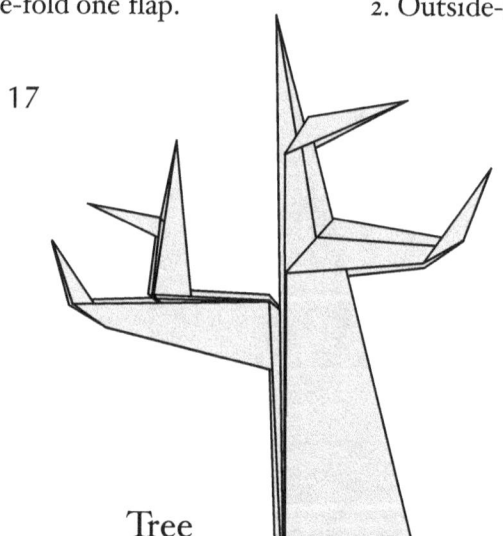

Tree

18 *Origami Twelve Days of Christmas*

Turtle Dove

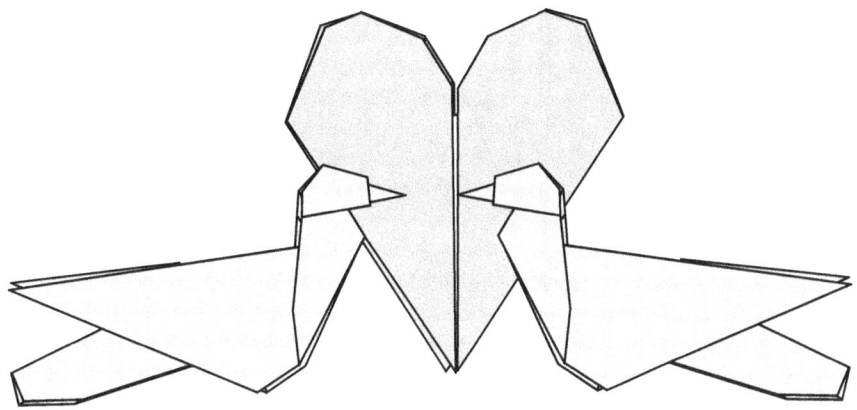

On the second day of Christmas,
my true love sent to me
Two turtle doves,
And a partridge in a pear tree.

1

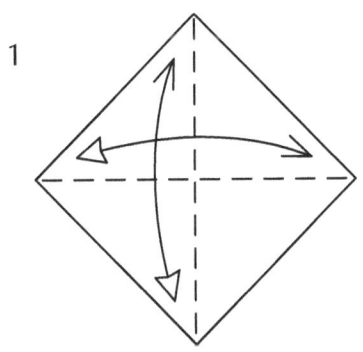

Fold and unfold.

2

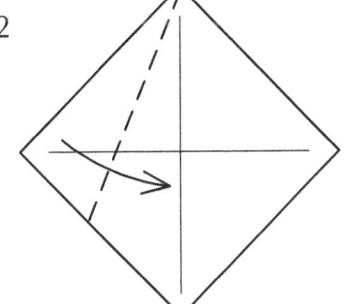

Fold to the center.

3

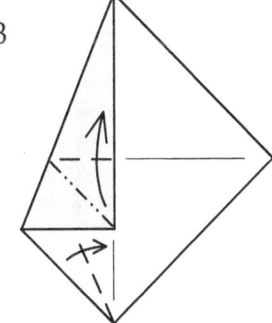

Squash-fold.

4

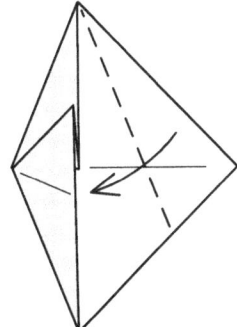

Repeat steps 2–3 on the right.

5

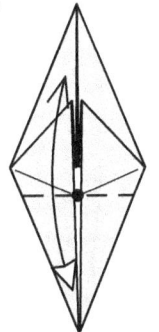

Fold and unfold.

6

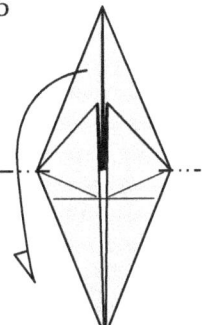

Fold behind.

7

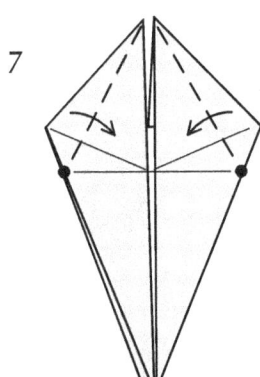

Turtle Dove 19

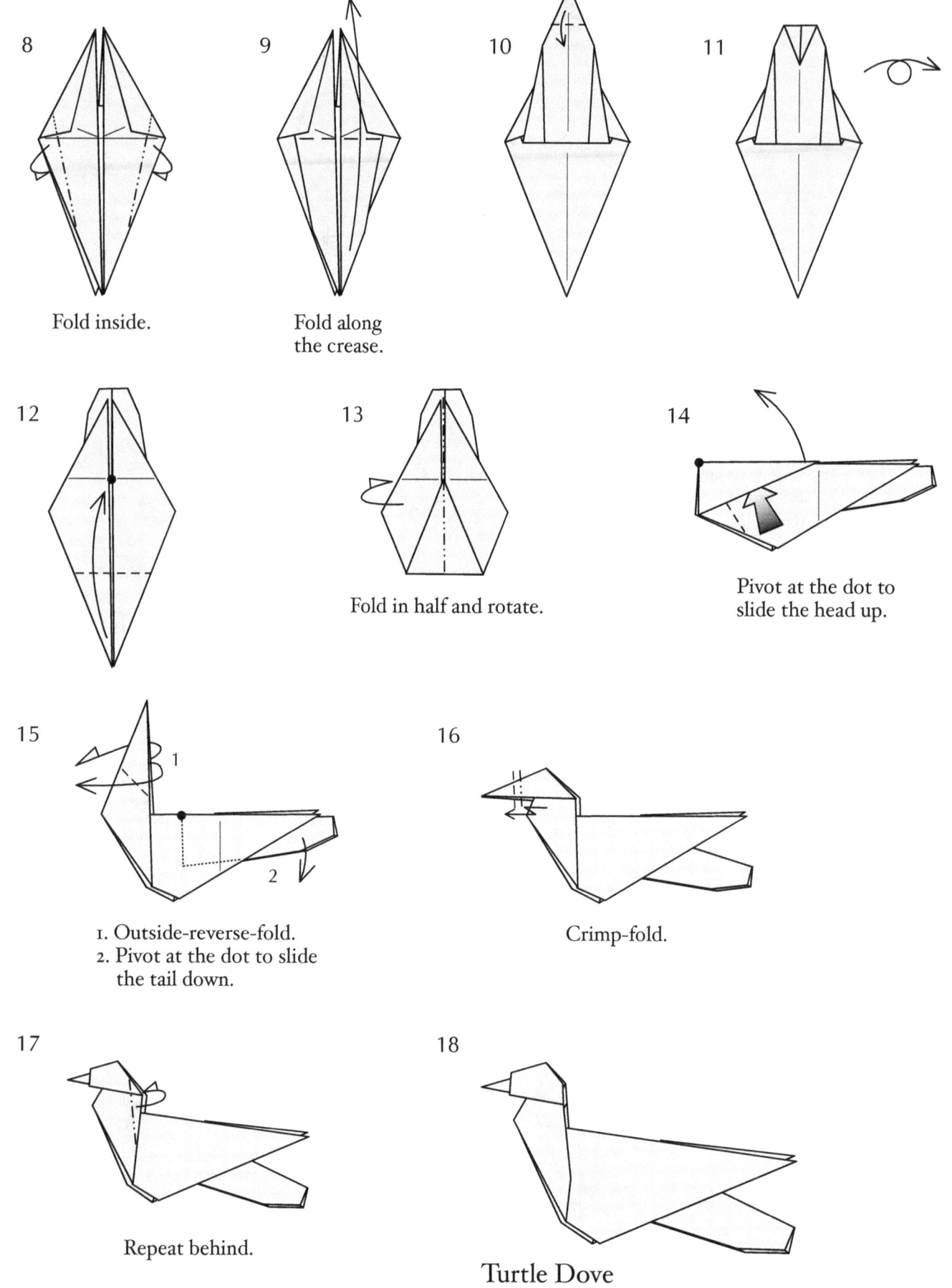

Heart

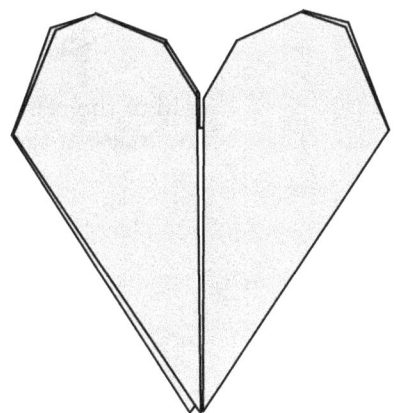

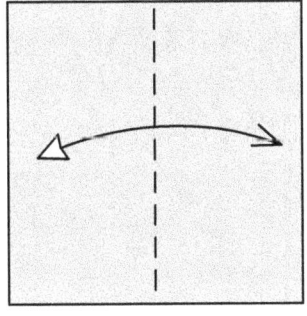
1. Fold and unfold.

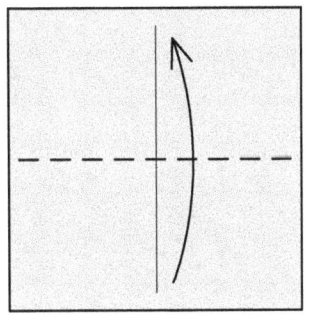
2. Fold in half.

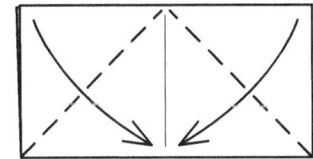
3. Fold the top layer.

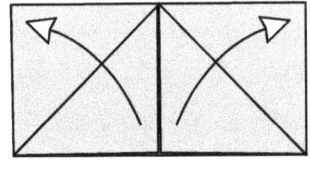
4. Unfold.

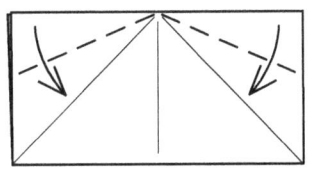
5. Fold the top layer.

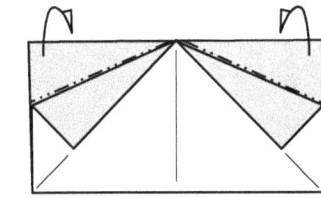
6. Fold behind.

Heart 21

7

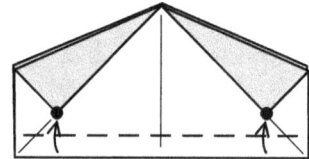

8

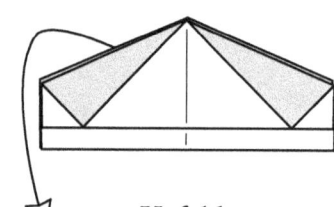

Unfold.

9

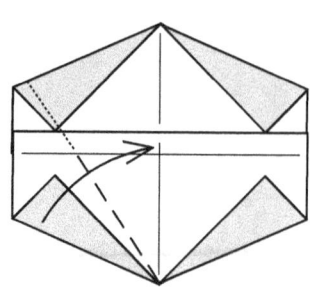

Fold to the center but do not crease at the top.

10

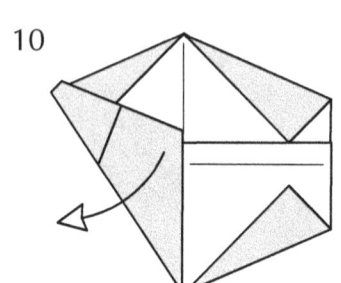

11

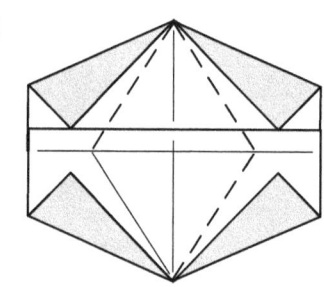

Repeat steps 9–10 three times.

12

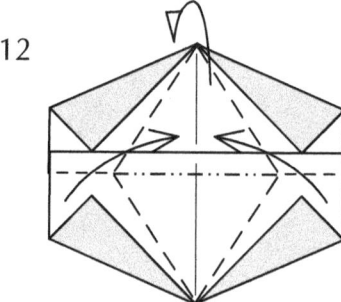

Fold along the creases.

13

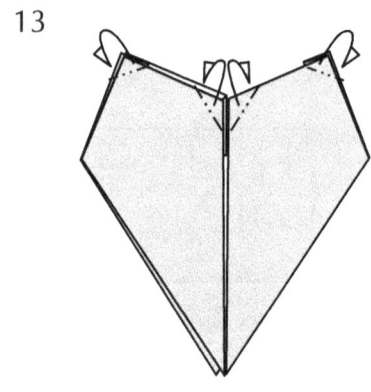

Fold inside. Repeat behind.

14

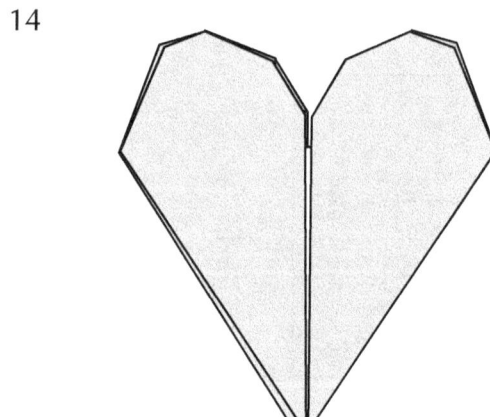

Heart

French Hen

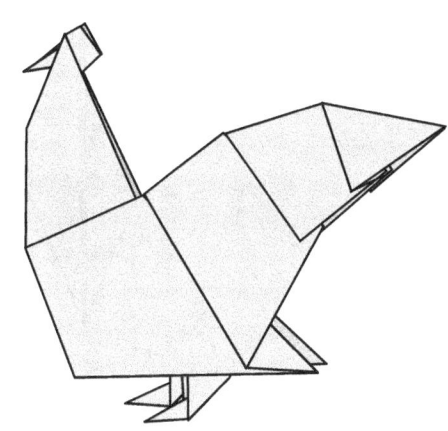

On the third day of Christmas,
my true love sent to me
Three French hens,
Two turtle doves,
And a partridge in a pear tree.

1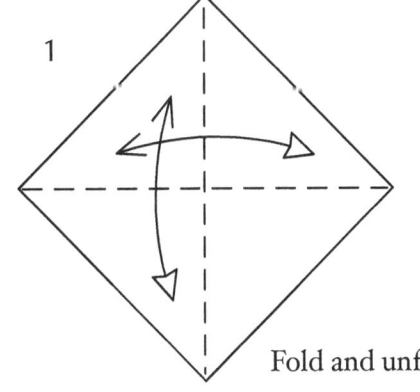
Fold and unfold.

2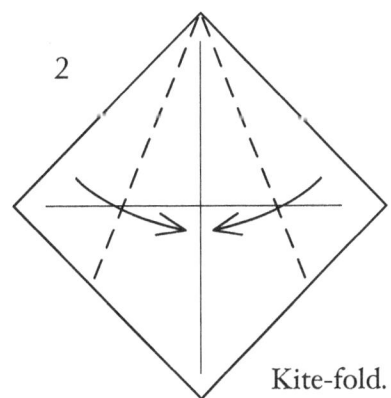
Kite-fold.

3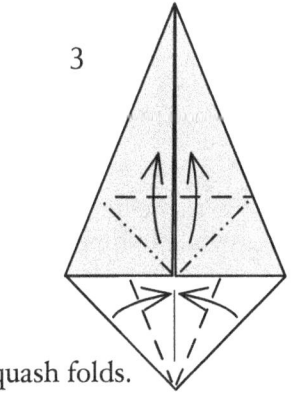
Squash folds.

4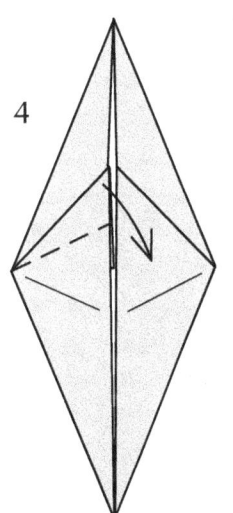

5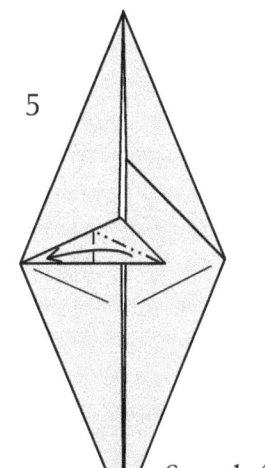
Squash-fold.

6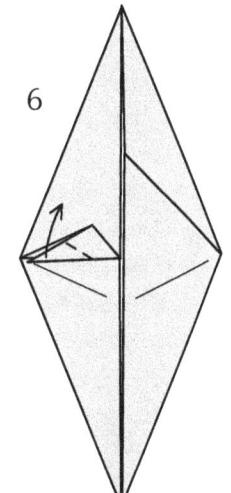

7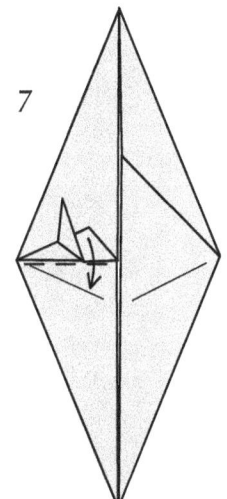

French Hen 23

8

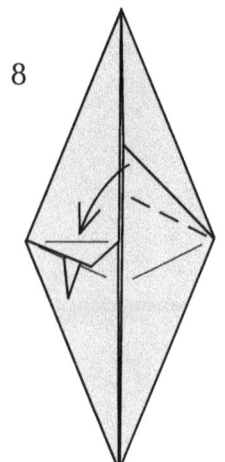

Repeat steps 4–7 on the right.

9

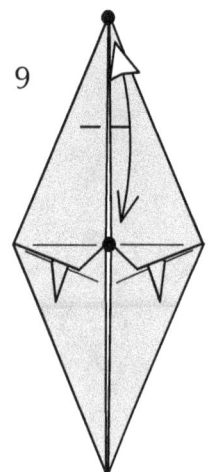

Fold and unfold.

10

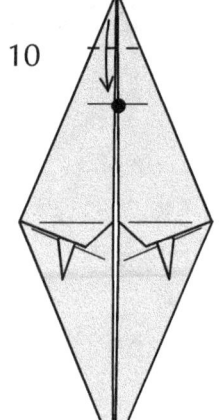

11

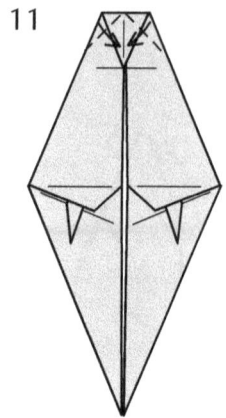

12

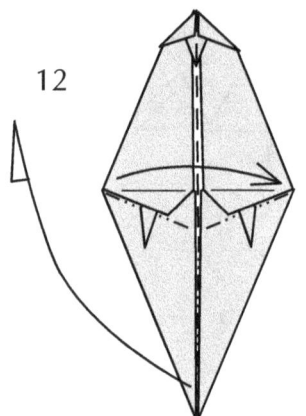

Lift the bottom up while folding in half.

13

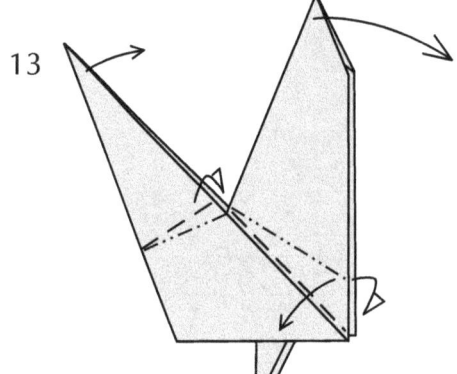

Crimp-fold inside for the neck and crimp-fold outside for the tail.

14

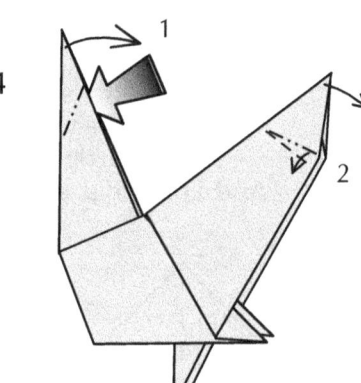

1. Reverse-fold.
2. Crimp-fold.

15

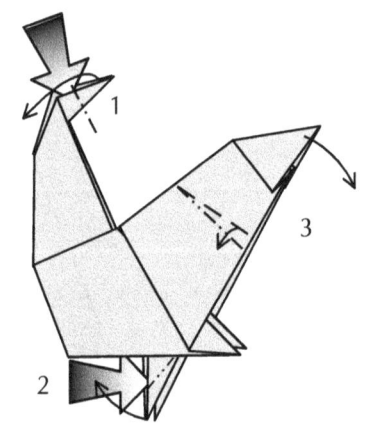

1. Reverse-fold.
2. Reverse-fold, repeat behind.
3. Crimp-fold.

16

French Hen

24 *Origami Twelve Days of Christmas*

Calling Bird

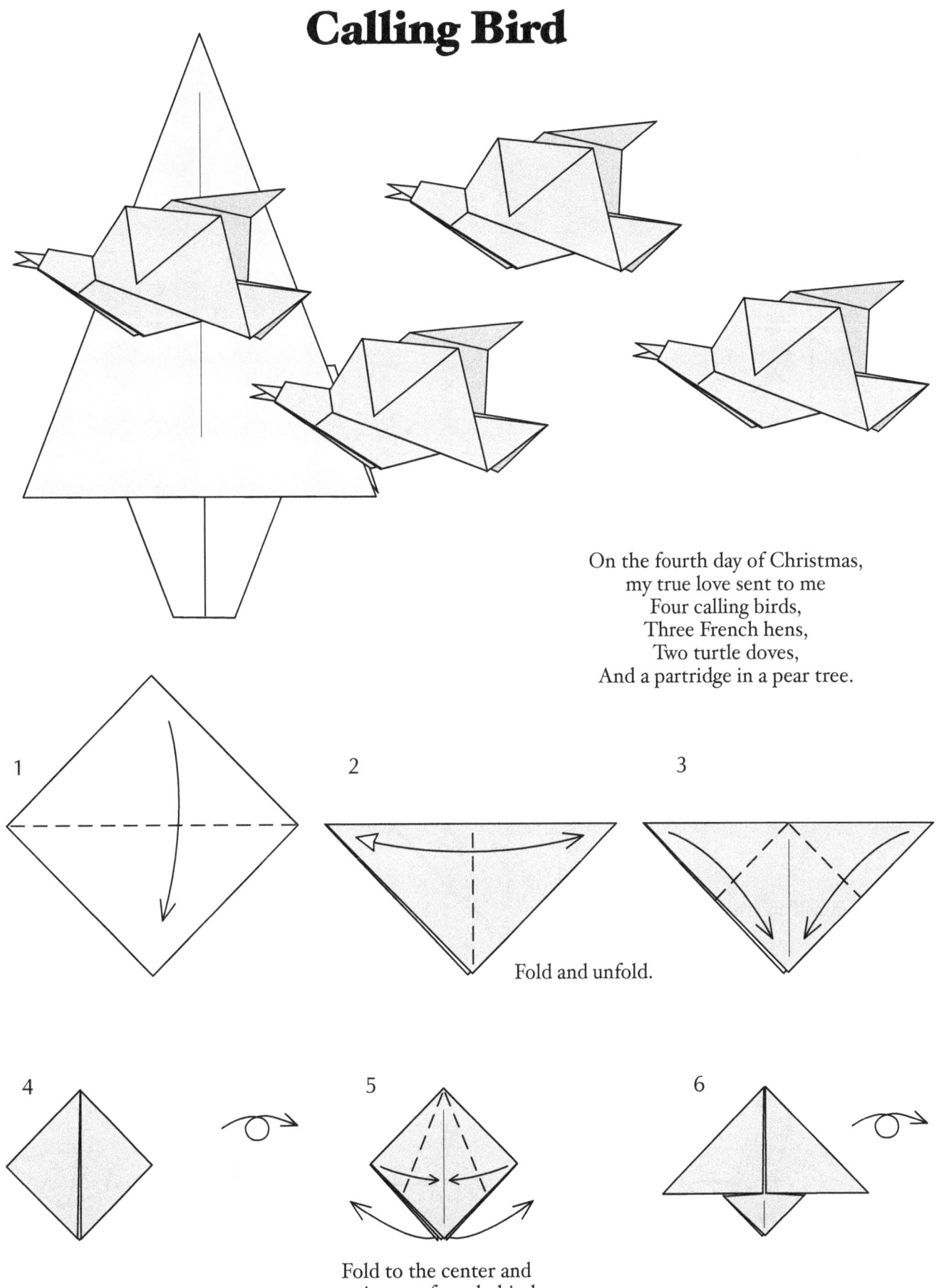

On the fourth day of Christmas,
my true love sent to me
Four calling birds,
Three French hens,
Two turtle doves,
And a partridge in a pear tree.

1.

2. Fold and unfold.

3.

4.

5. Fold to the center and swing out from behind.

6.

Calling Bird 25

7

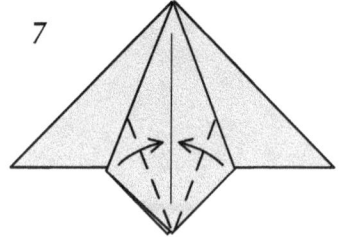

8

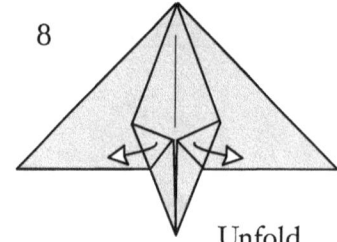

Unfold.

9

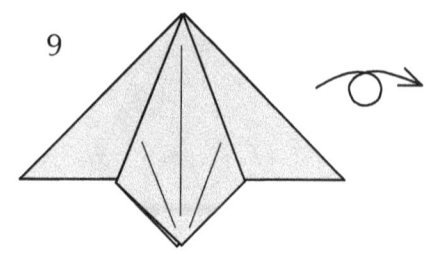

10

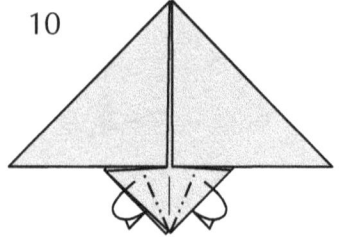

Fold inside.

11

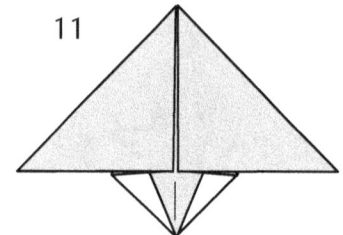

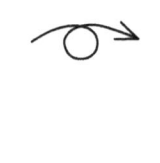

12

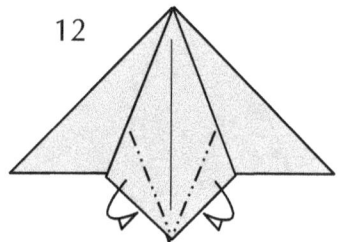

Reverse-fold the paper inside.

13

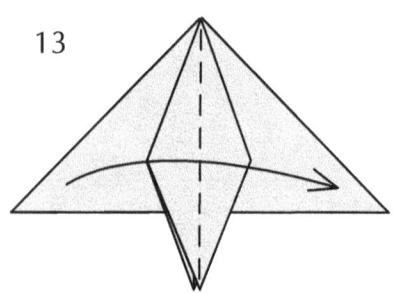

Fold in half and rotate.

14

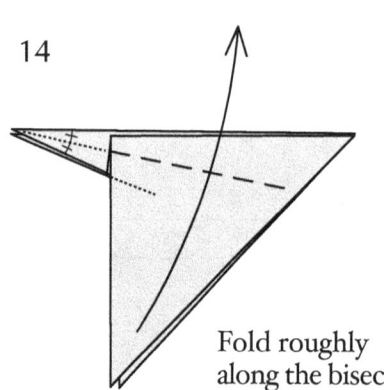

Fold roughly along the bisector. Repeat behind.

15

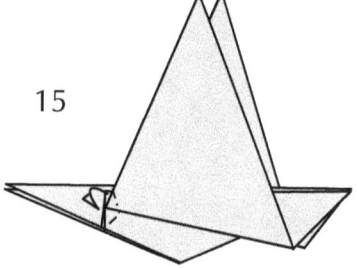

Fold behind. Repeat behind.

16

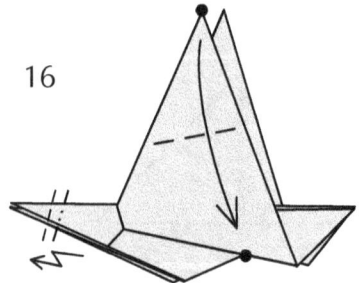

Crimp-fold the beak. Repeat behind at the wing.

17

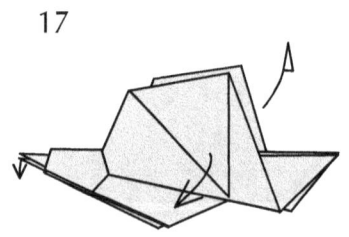

Spread the wings and beak.

18

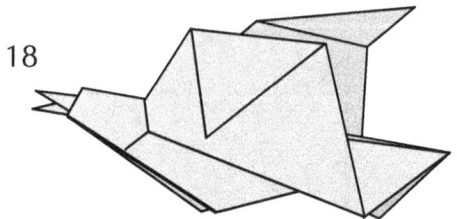

Calling Bird

26 *Origami Twelve Days of Christmas*

Christmas Tree

Traditional

1. Fold and unfold.
2. Kite-fold.
3. 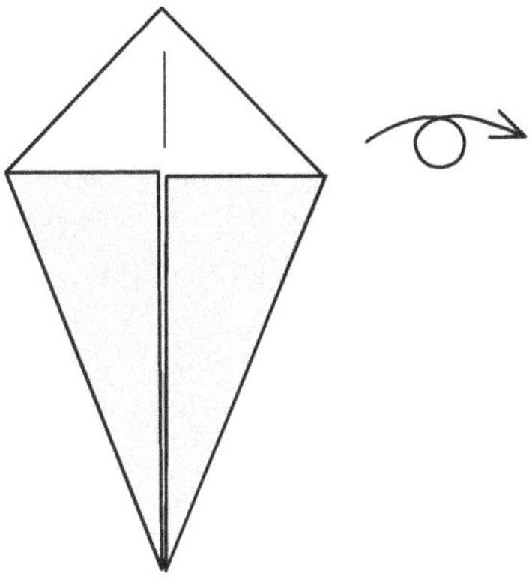
4. 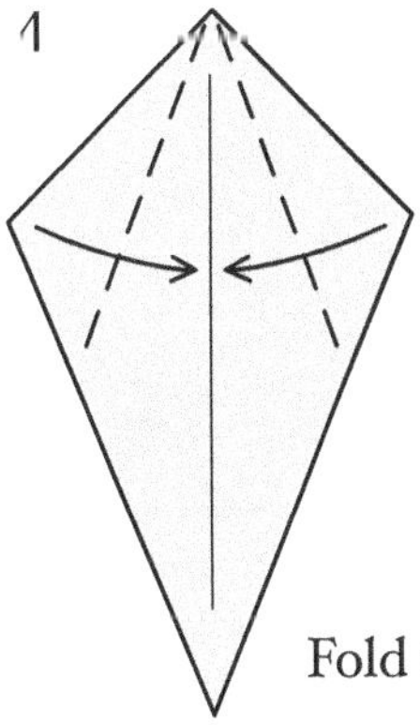 Fold to the center.
5. 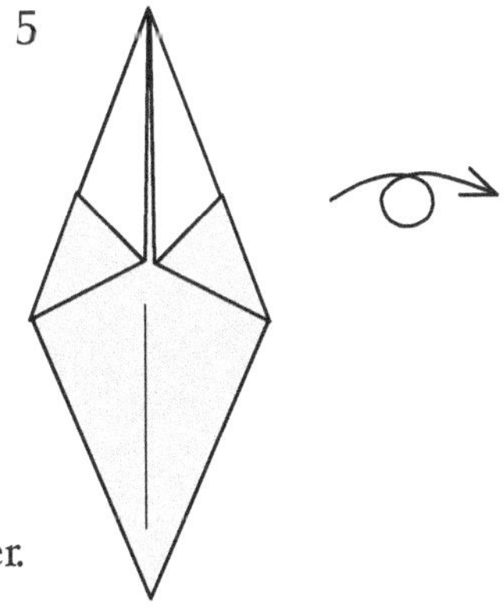
6. 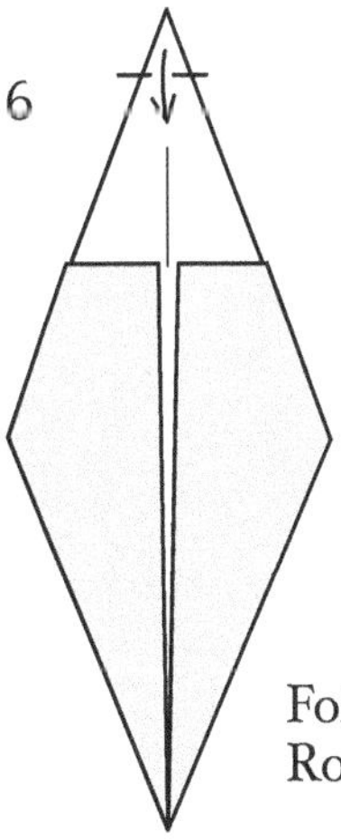 Fold down. Rotate 180°.
7. Fold up.

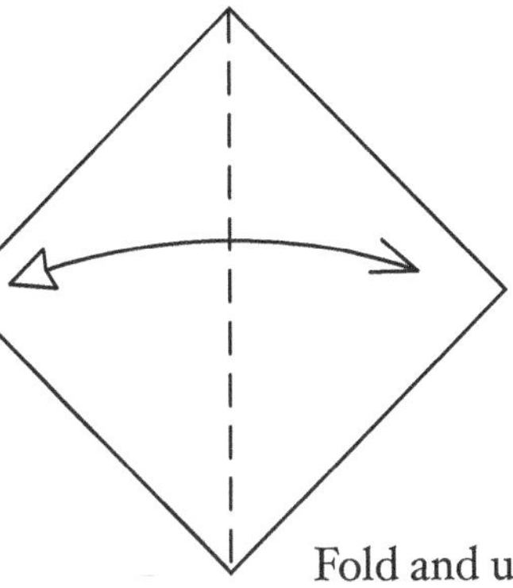

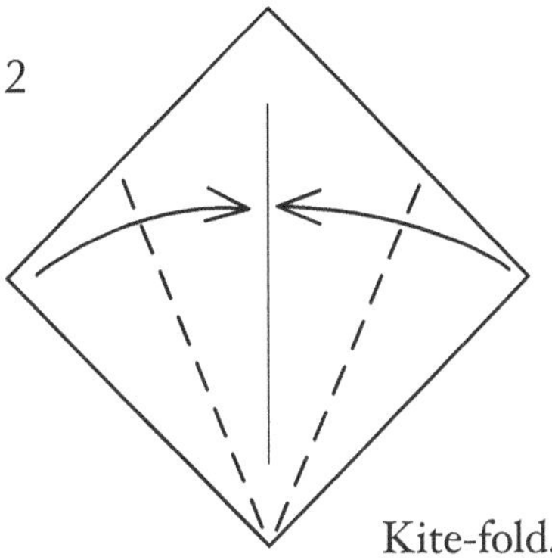

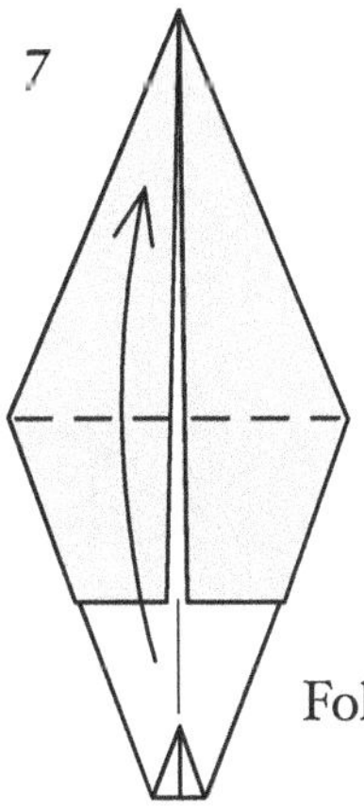

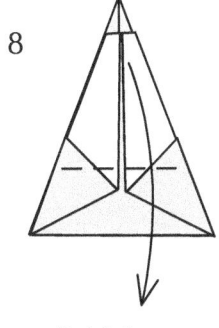

8. Fold down.

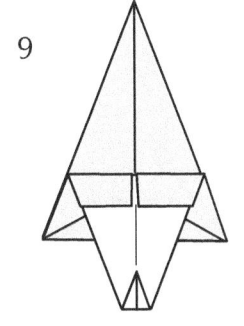

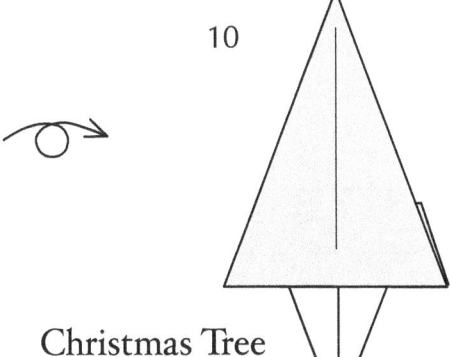

10. Christmas Tree

Christmas Tree 27

Golden Ring

On the fifth day of Christmas,
my true love sent to me
Five golden rings,
Four calling birds,
Three French hens,
Two turtle doves,
And a partridge in a pear tree.

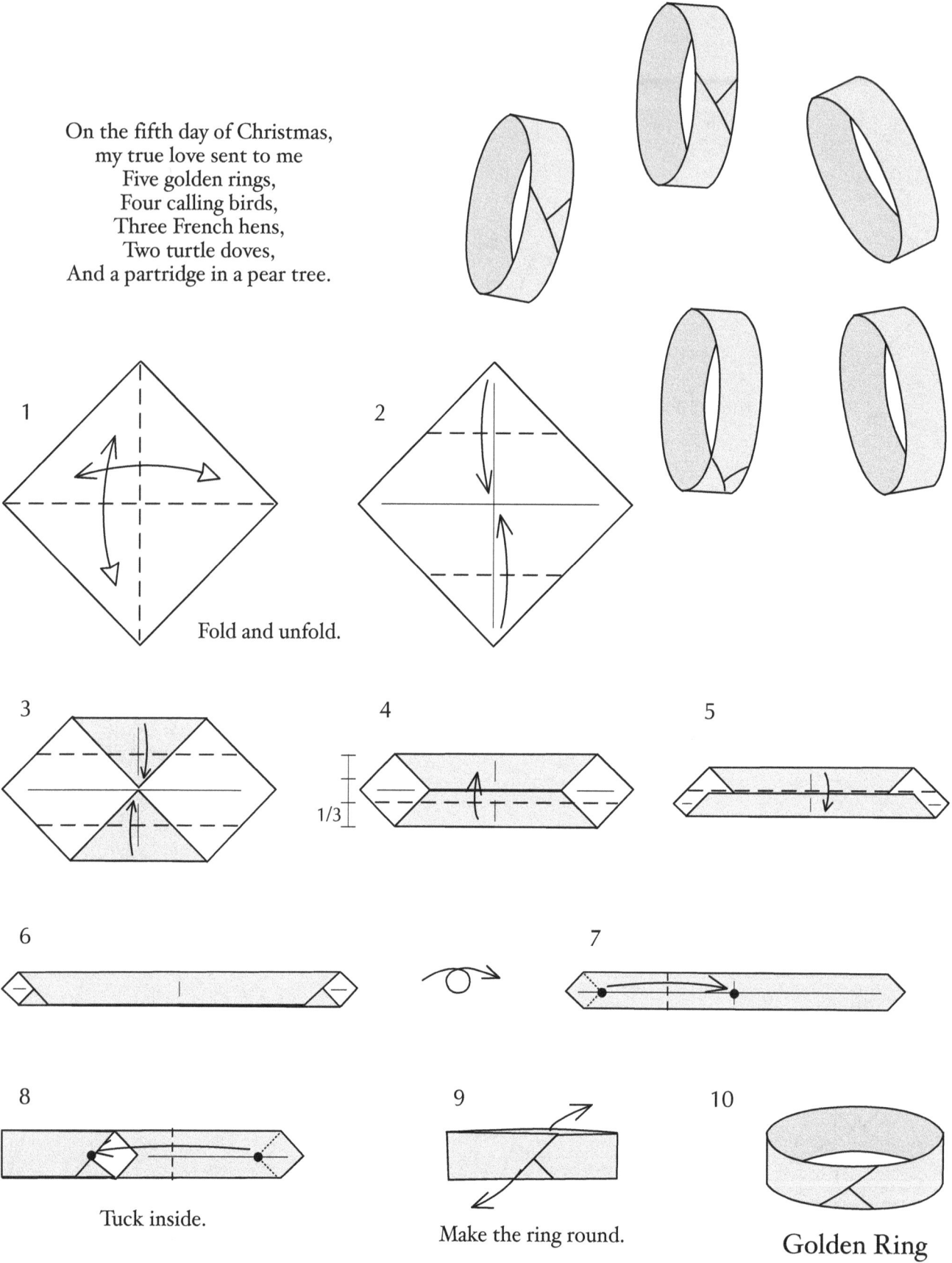

1. Fold and unfold.
2.
3.
4. 1/3
5.
6.
7.
8. Tuck inside.
9. Make the ring round.
10. Golden Ring

28 *Origami Twelve Days of Christmas*

Goose

On the sixth day of Christmas,
my true love sent to me
Six geese a-laying,
Five golden rings,
Four calling birds,
Three French hens,
Two turtle doves,
And a partridge in a pear tree.

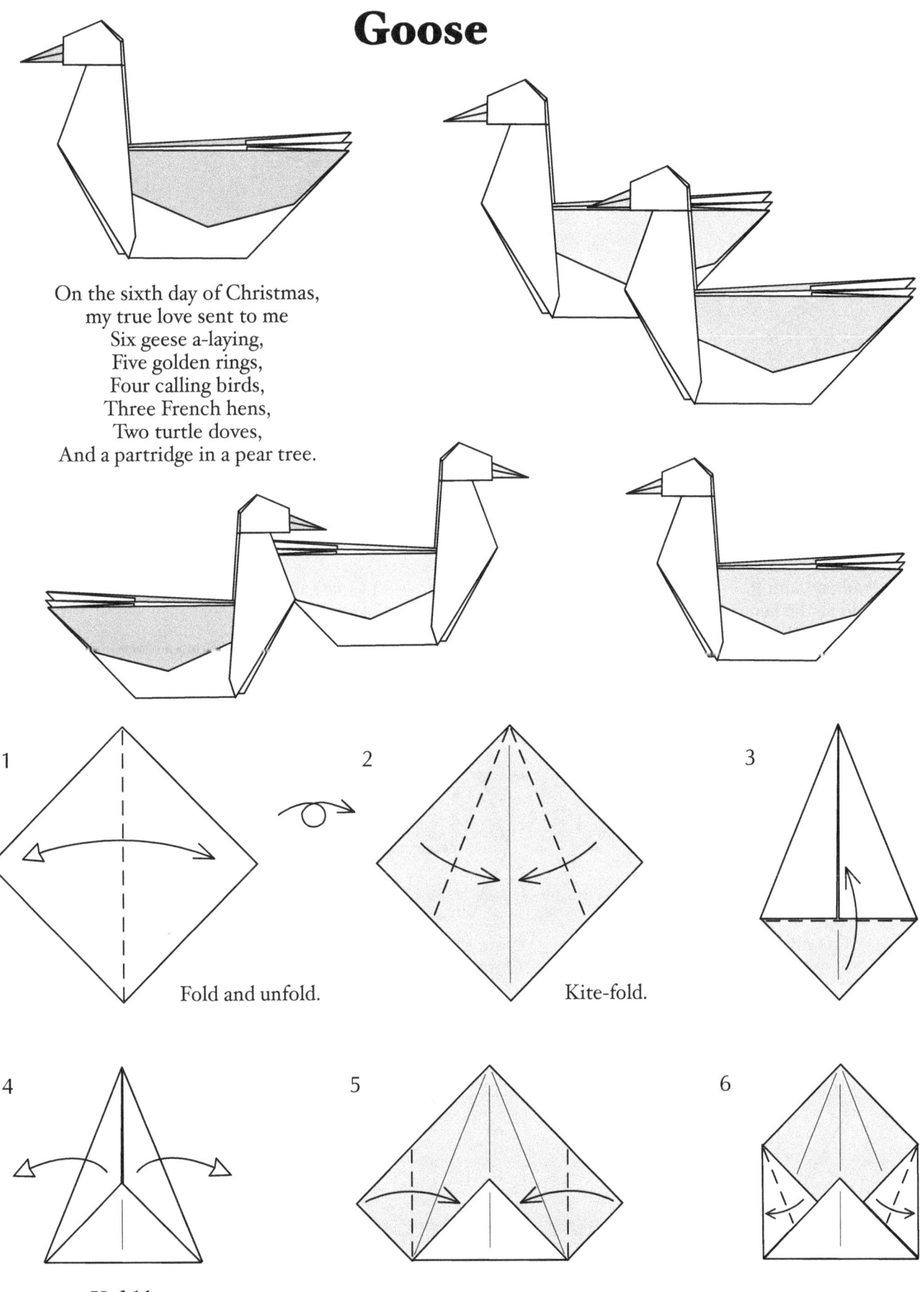

1. Fold and unfold.
2. Kite-fold.
3.
4. Unfold.
5.
6.

Goose 29

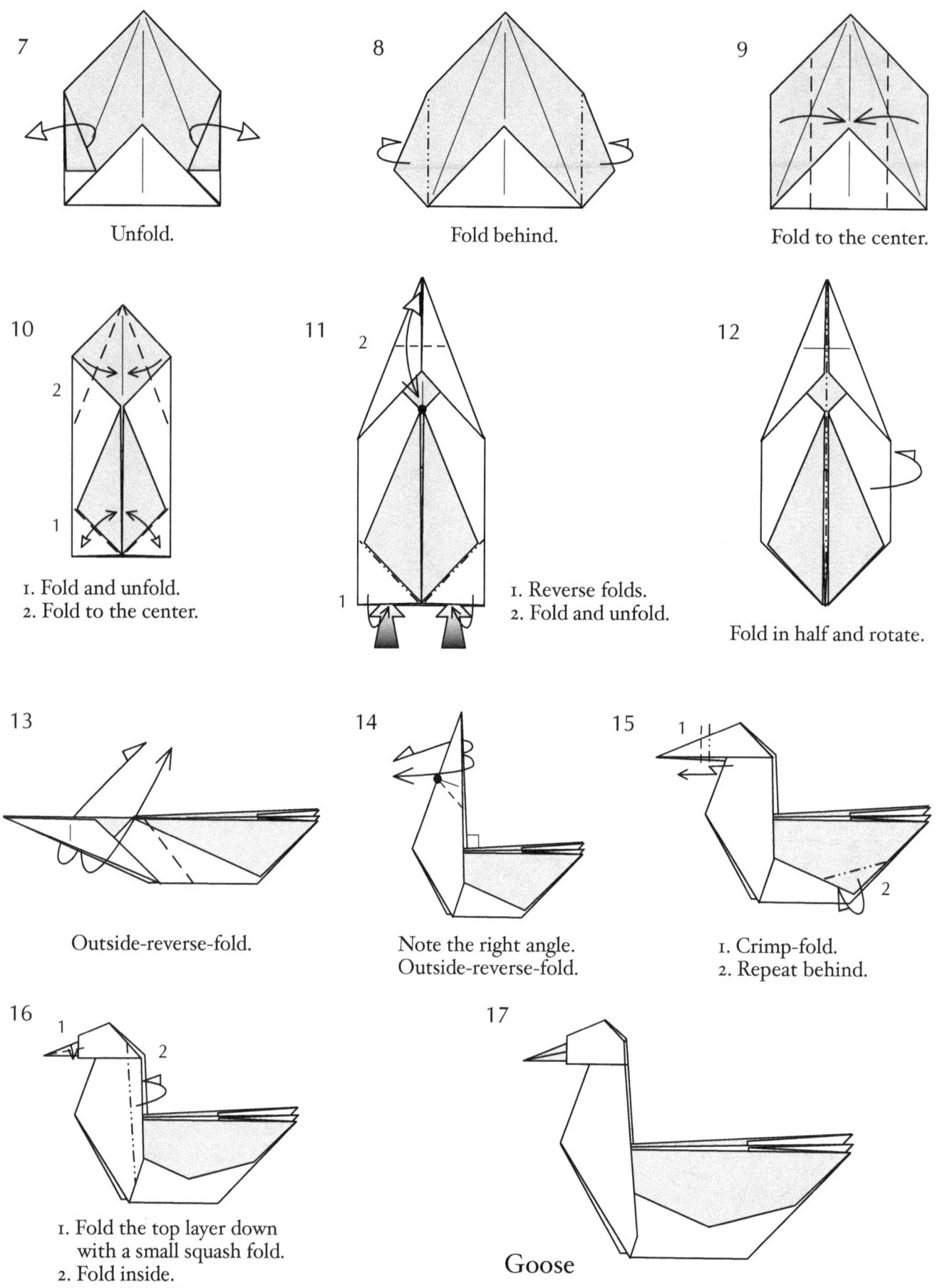

Swan

On the seventh day of Christmas,
my true love sent to me
Seven swans a-swimming,
Six geese a-laying,
Five golden rings,
Four calling birds,
Three French hens,
Two turtle doves,
And a partridge in a pear tree.

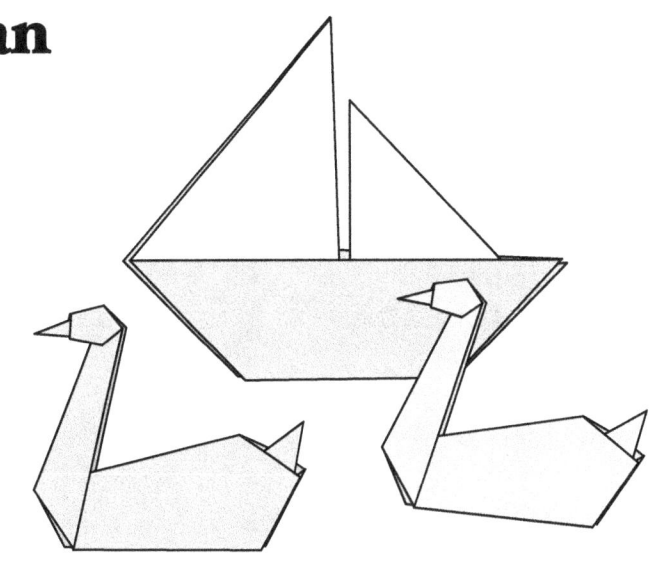

1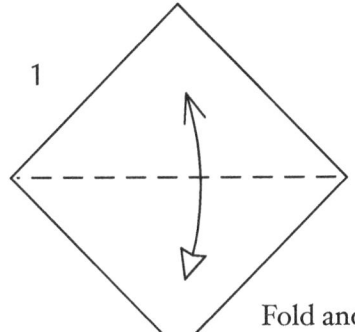

Fold and unfold.

2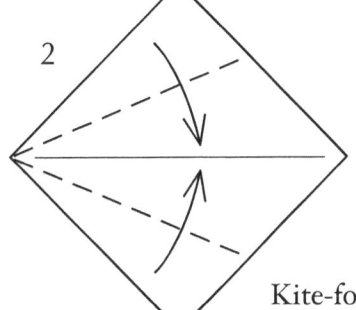

Kite-fold.

3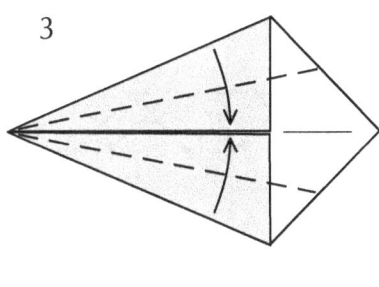

4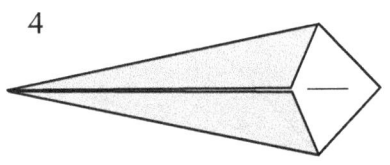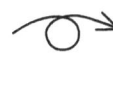

5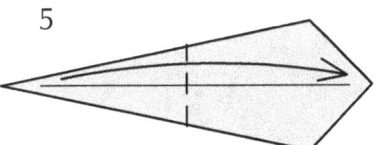

6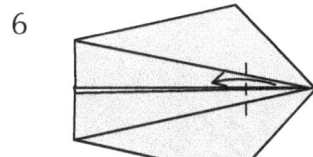

7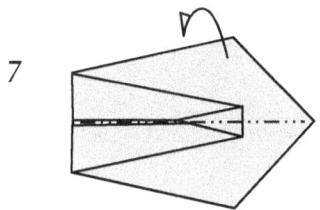

8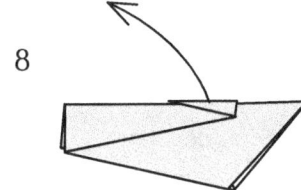

Lift up the neck and head.

9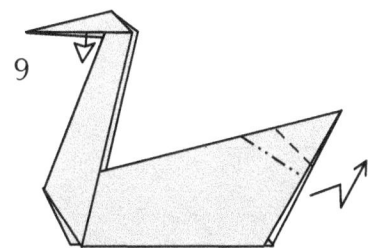

Pull out at the head and repeat behind. Crimp-fold the tail.

10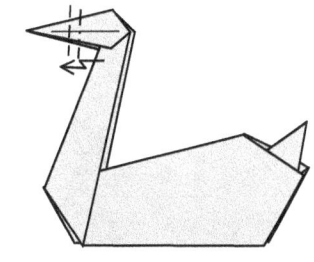

Crimp-fold the beak.

11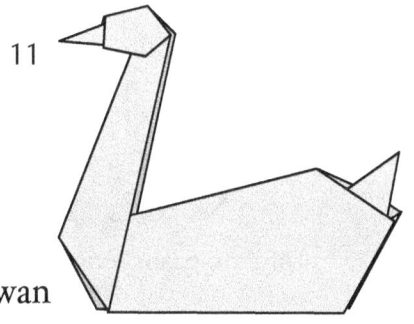

Swan

Sailboat

Traditional

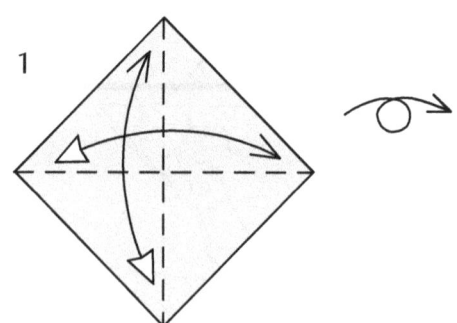

1. Fold and unfold.

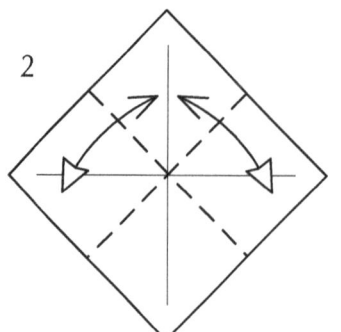

2. Fold and unfold.

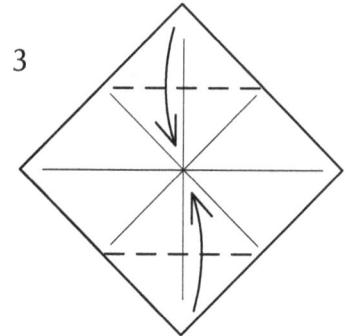

3. Fold opposite corners to the center.

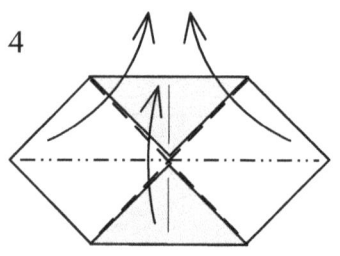

4. Fold along the creases.

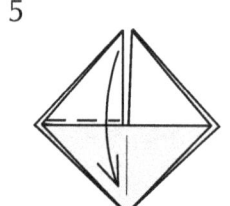

5. Fold one side down.

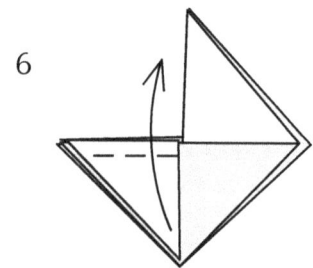

6. Fold up.

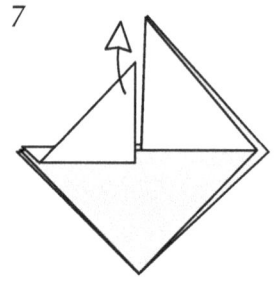

7. Unfold.

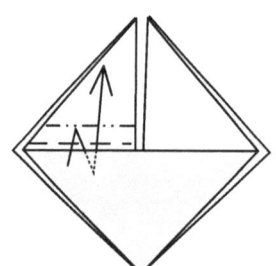

8. Refold while tucking inside.

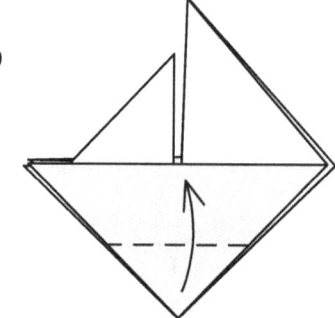

9. Fold up.

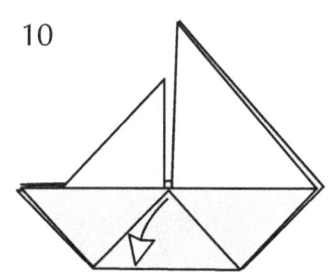

10. Fold the triangle down a little so the sailboat can stand.

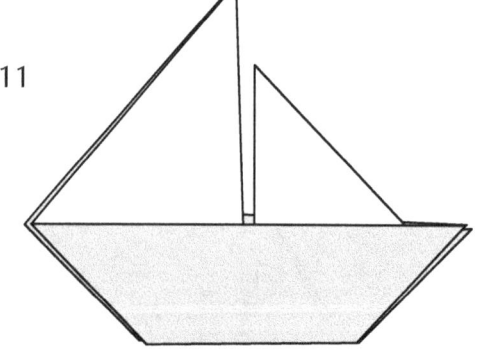

11. Sailboat

32 *Origami Twelve Days of Christmas*

Maids a-Milking

On the eighth day of Christmas,
my true love sent to me
Eight maids a-milking,
Seven swans a-swimming,
Six geese a-laying,
Five golden rings,
Four calling birds,
Three French hens,
Two turtle doves,
And a partridge in a pear tree.

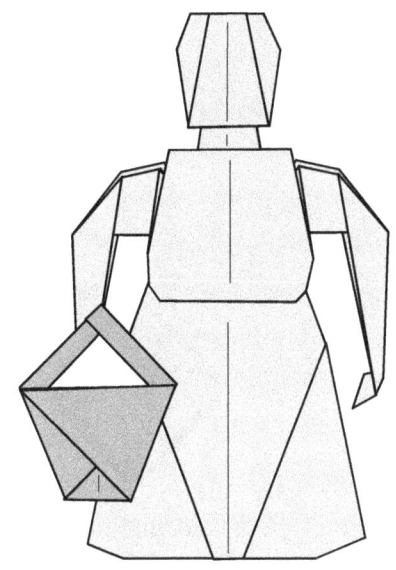

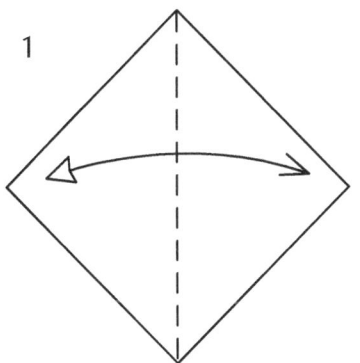

1

Fold and unfold.

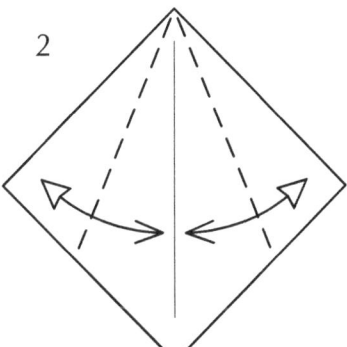

2

Kite-fold and unfold.

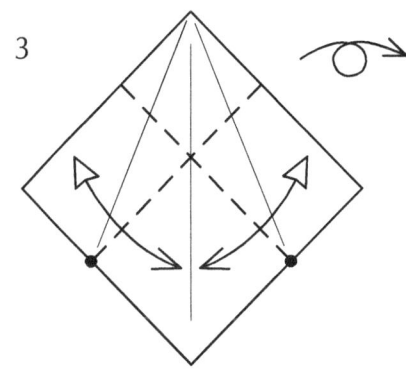

3

Fold and unfold.

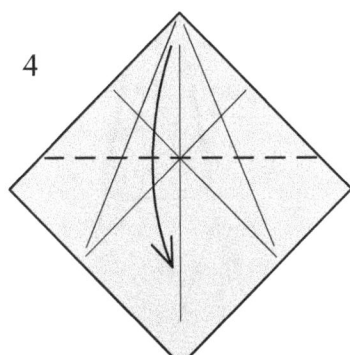

4

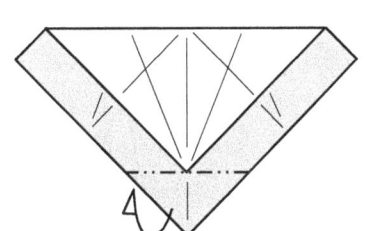

5

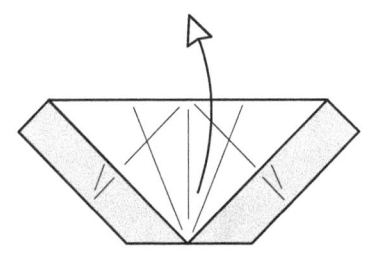

6

Unfold.

Maids a-Milking 33

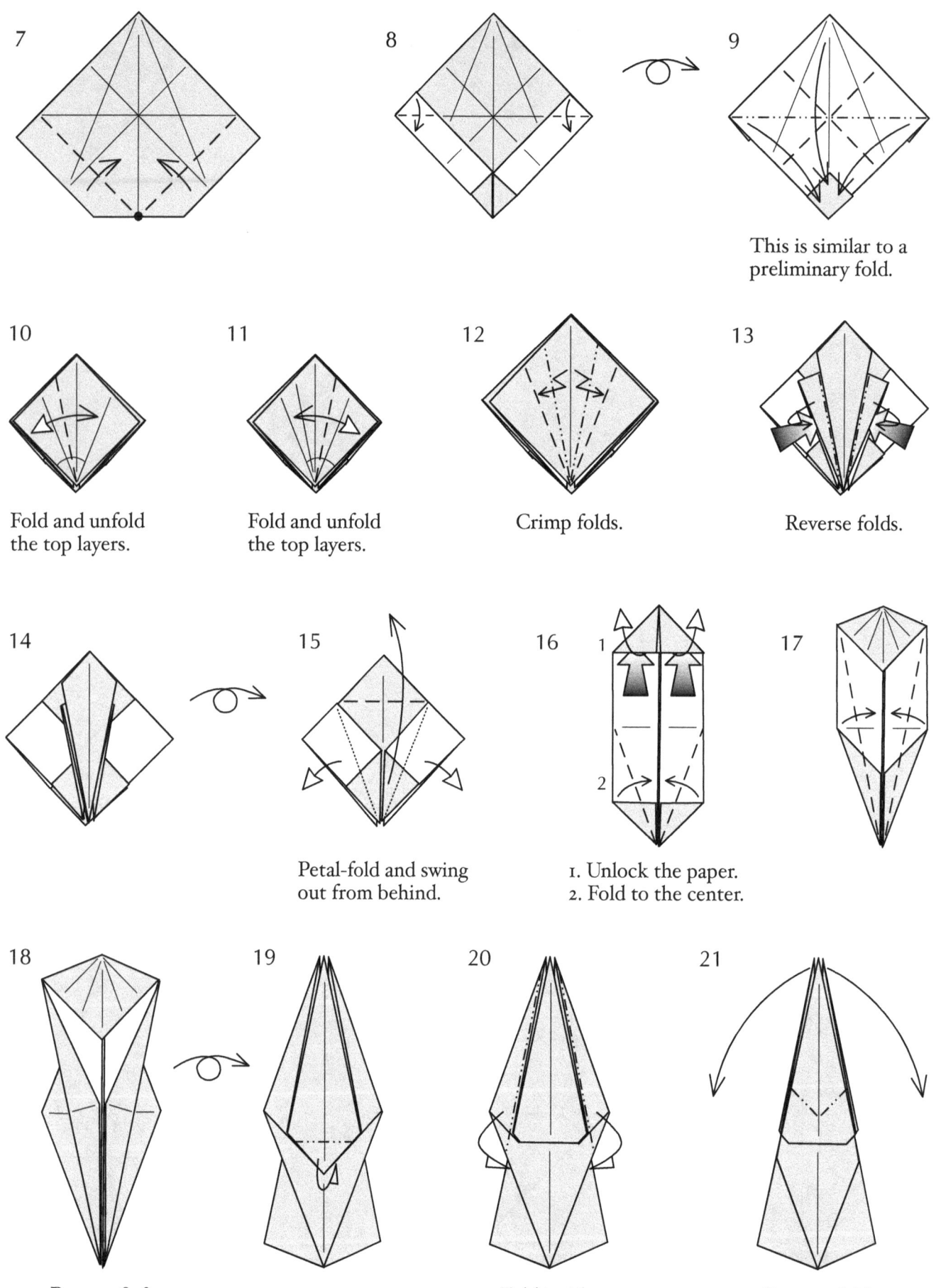

34 *Origami Twelve Days of Christmas*

22

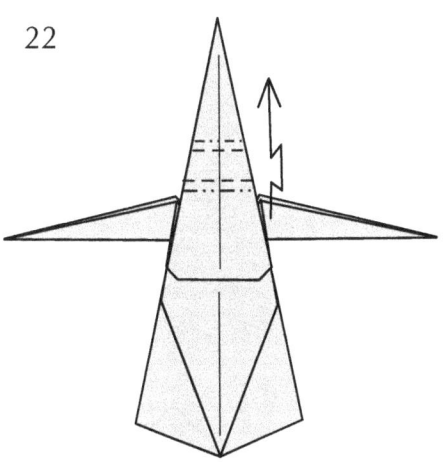

Pleat folds.

23

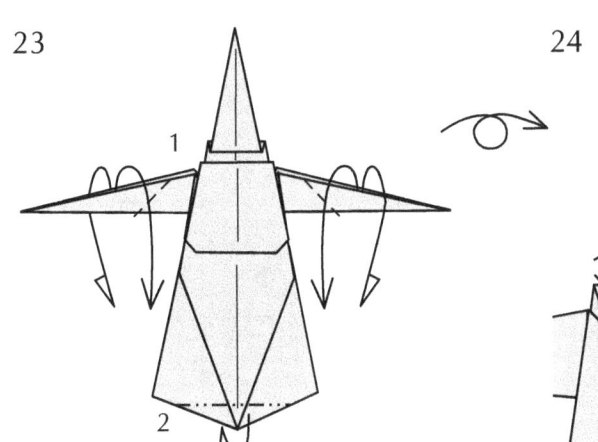

1. Outside-reverse folds.
2. Mountain-fold.

24

Thin petal folds.

25

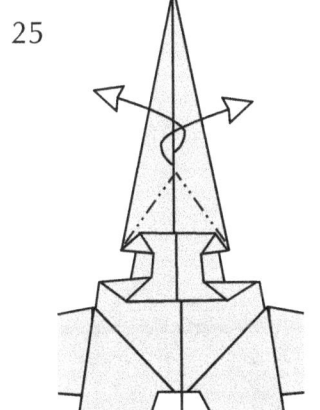

Spread the top layer.

26

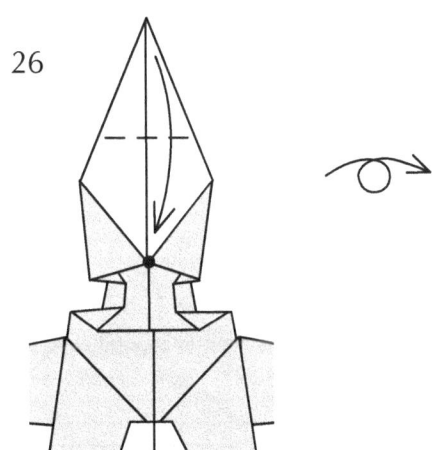

27

Spread the hands and shape the model.

28

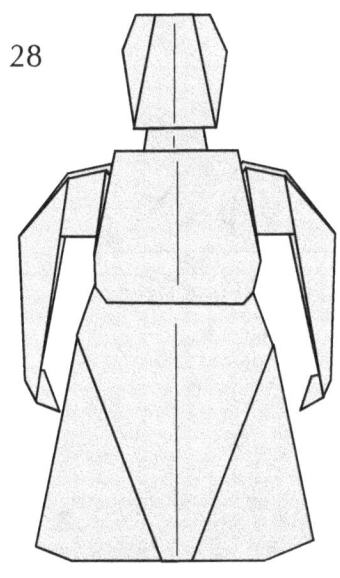

Maid a-Milking

Pail

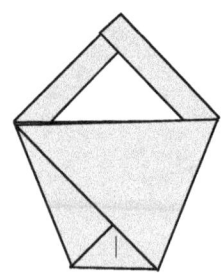
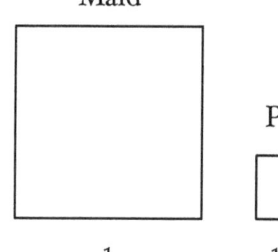

Maid — 1
Pail — 1/3

1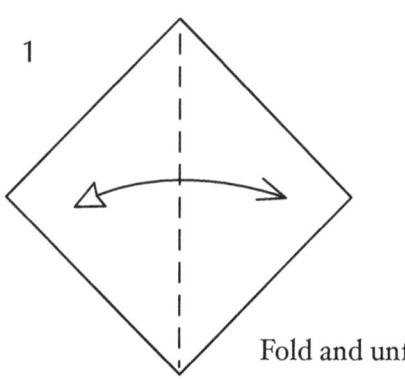
Fold and unfold.

2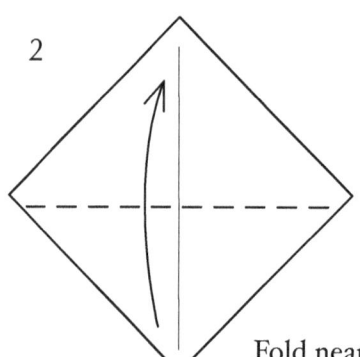
Fold near the top.

3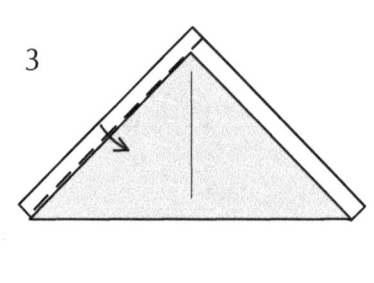

4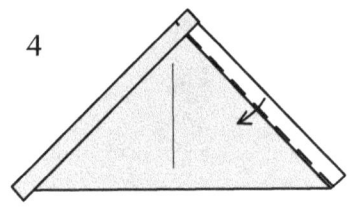

5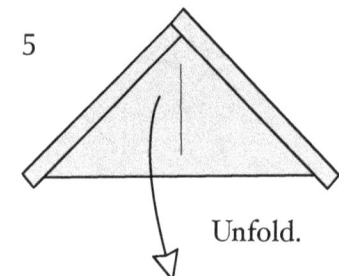
Unfold.

6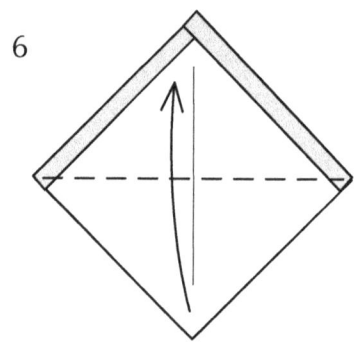

7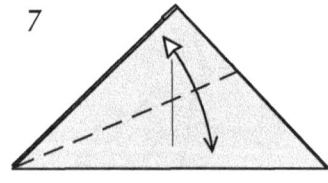
Fold and unfold one layer.

8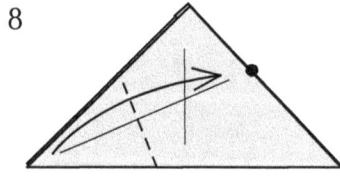

9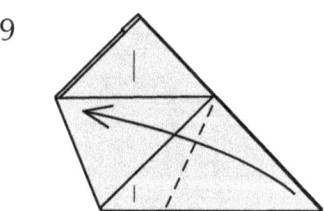

10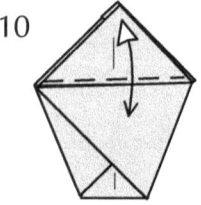
Fold and unfold one layer.

11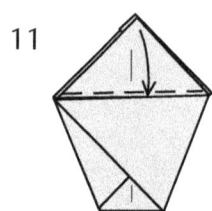
Tuck inside the pocket.

12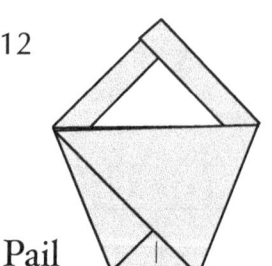
Pail

36 *Origami Twelve Days of Christmas*

Ladies Dancing

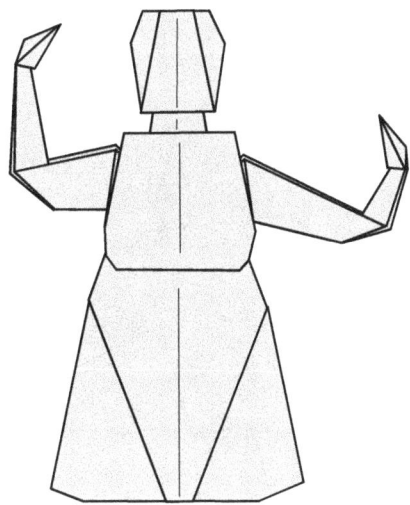
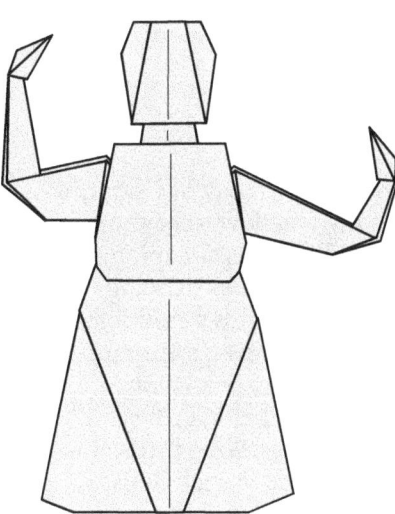

On the ninth day of Christmas,
my true love sent to me
Nine ladies dancing,
Eight maids a-milking,
Seven swans a-swimming,
Six geese a-laying,
Five golden rings,
Four calling birds,
Three French hens,
Two turtle doves,
And a partridge in a pear tree.

1

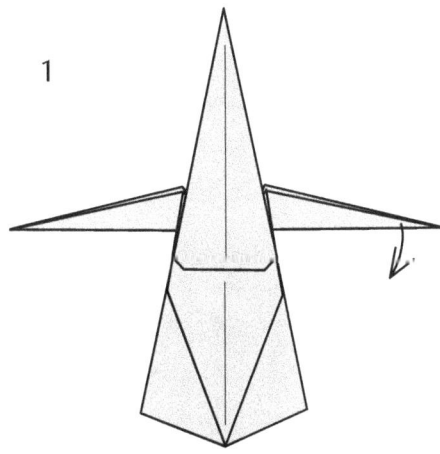

Begin with step 22 of the Maid a-Milking (page 33). Slide the arm.

2

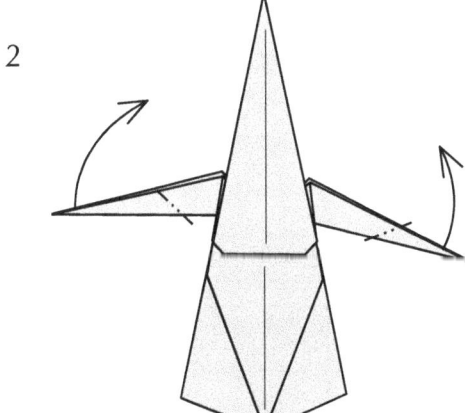

Reverse folds.

3

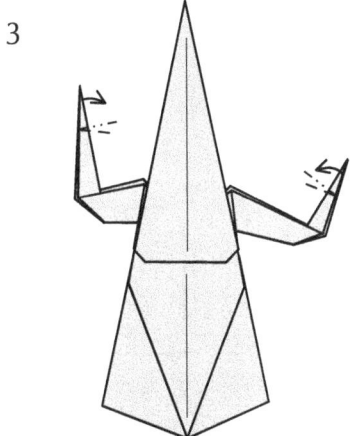

Make squash folds. Continue with steps 22 through the end of the Maid, but skips the steps about the arms.

4

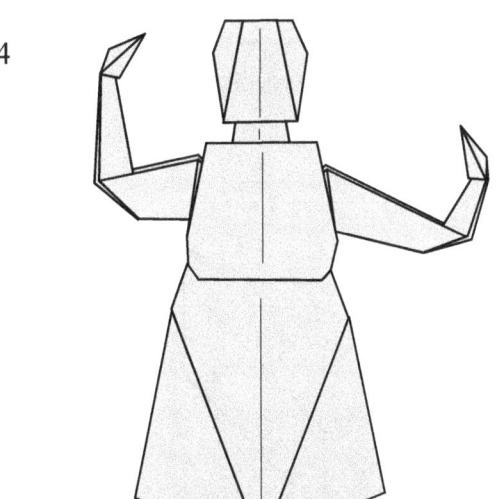

Lady Dancing

Lords a-Leaping

On the tenth day of Christmas,
my true love sent to me
Ten lords a-leaping,
Nine ladies dancing,
Eight maids a-milking,
Seven swans a-swimming,
Six geese a-laying,
Five golden rings,
Four calling birds,
Three French hens,
Two turtle doves,
And a partridge in a pear tree.

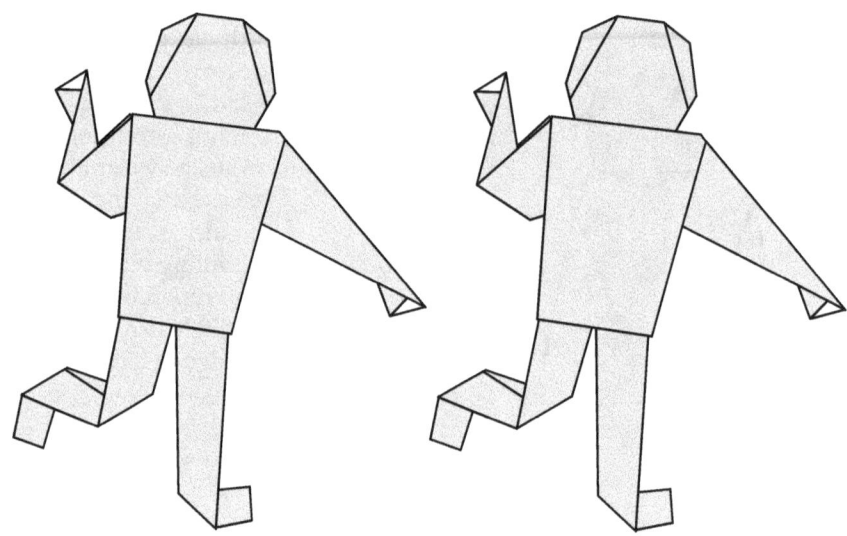

1

Fold and unfold.

2

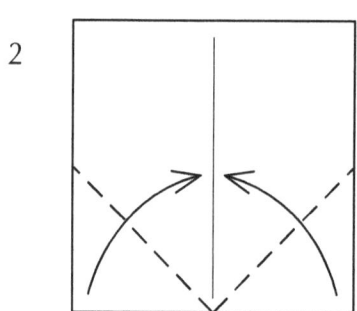

3

4

Unfold.

5

Repeat steps 3–4 in the opposite direction.

6

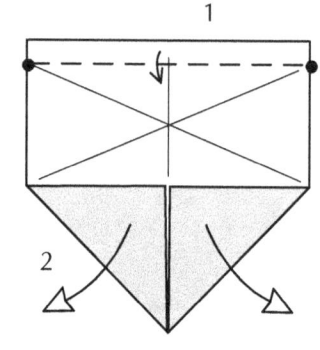

1. Valley-fold.
2. Unfold.

38 *Origami Twelve Days of Christmas*

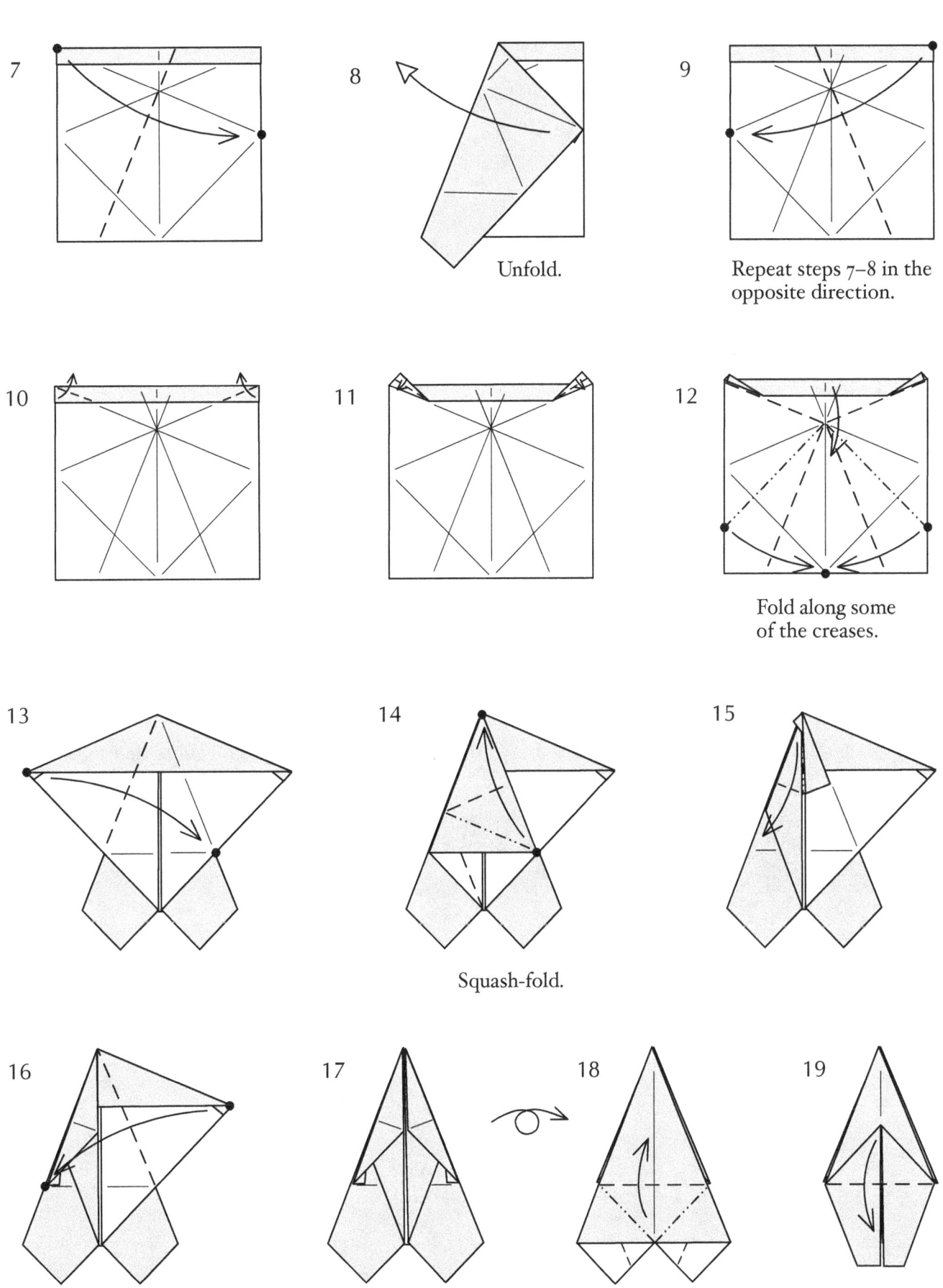

Lords a-Leaping 39

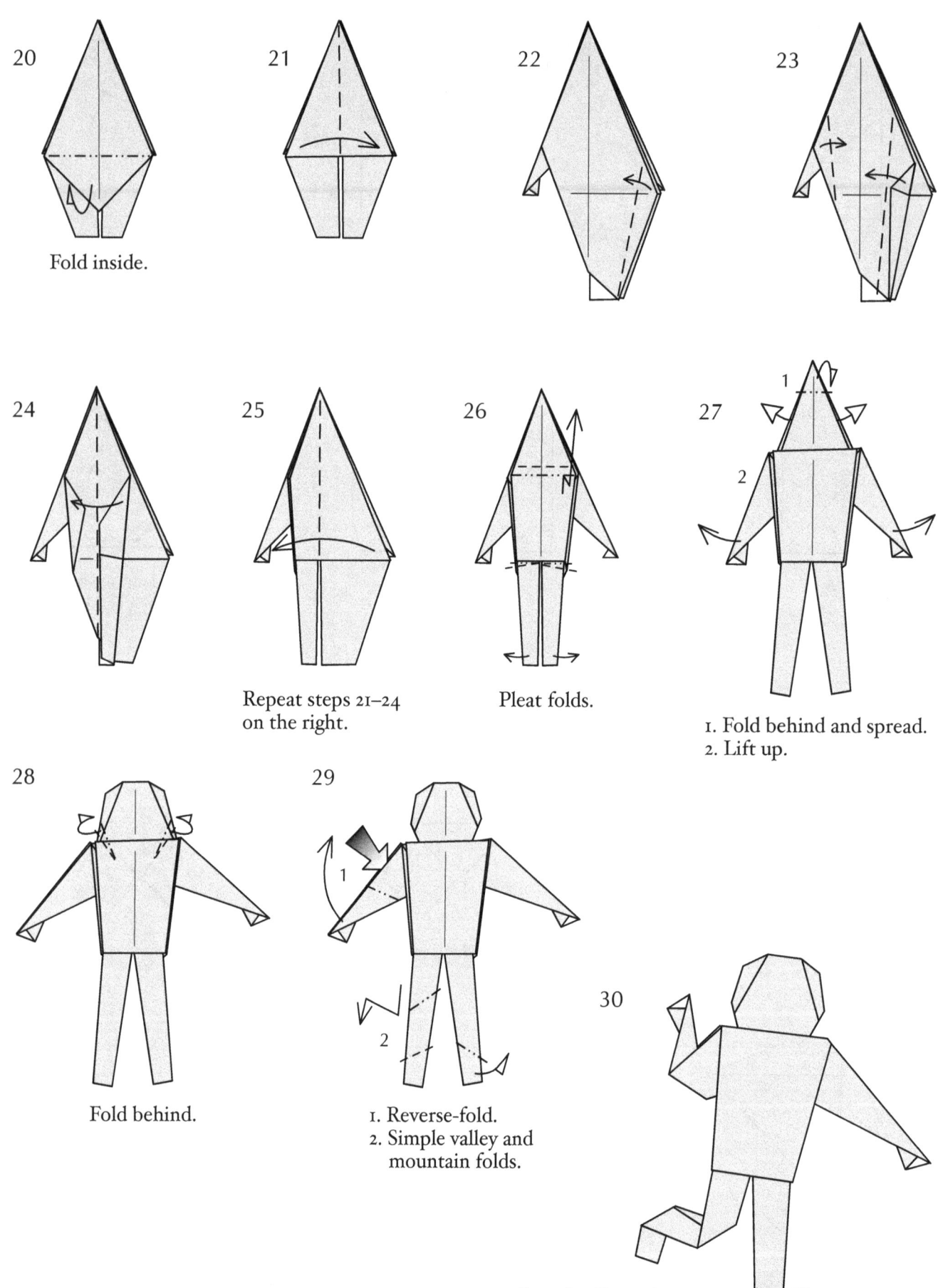

Pipers Piping

On the eleventh day of Christmas,
my true love sent to me
Eleven pipers piping,
Ten lords a-leaping,
Nine ladies dancing,
Eight maids a-milking,
Seven swans a-swimming,
Six geese a-laying,
Five golden rings,
Four calling birds,
Three French hens,
Two turtle doves,
And a partridge in a pear tree.

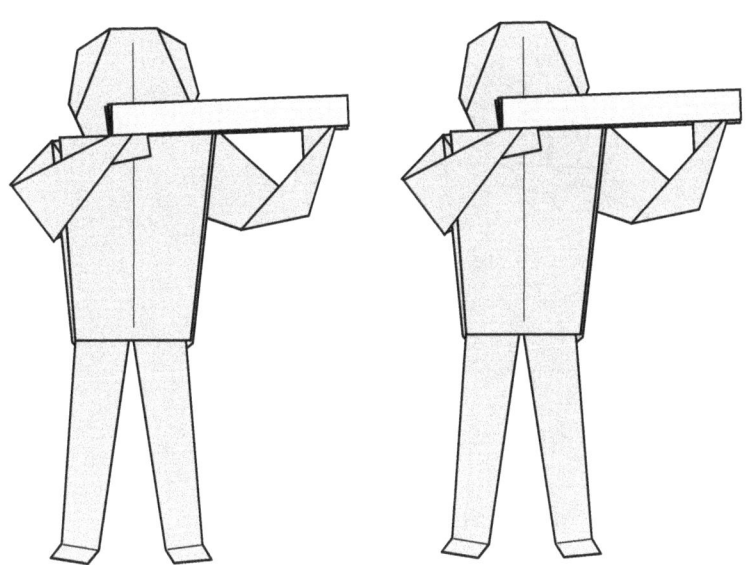

1

Begin with step 29 of the Lord a-Leaping (page 38). Make valley folds.

2

Piper Piping

Pipe

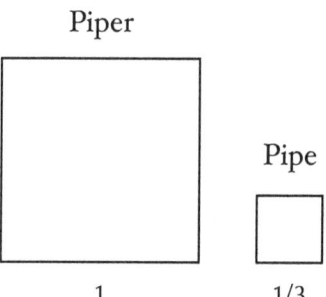

Piper
1

Pipe
1/3

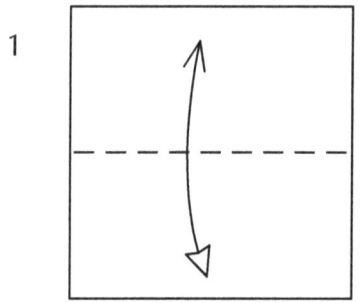

1. Fold and unfold.

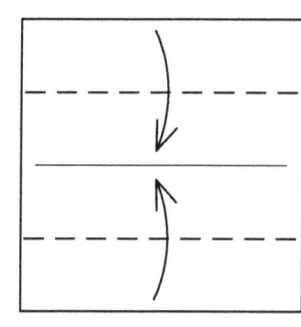

2. Fold to the center.

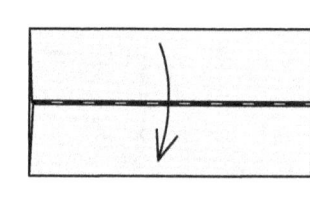

3. Fold in half.

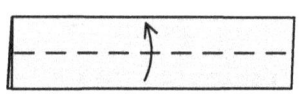

4. Repeat behind.

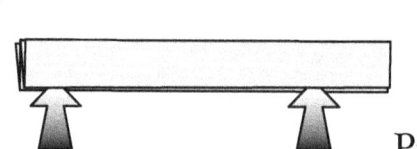

Pipe

5. Place the Piper's hands between the layers.

Drummers Drumming

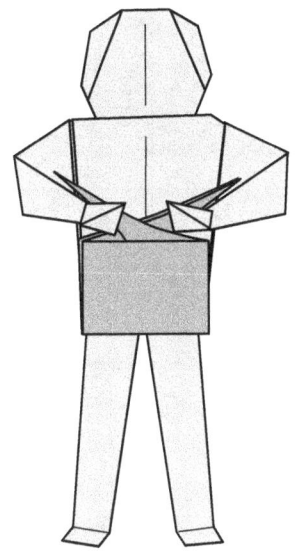 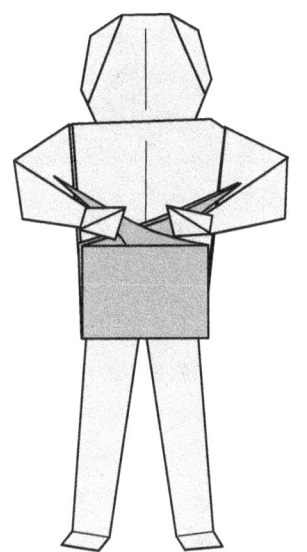

On the twelfth day of Christmas,
my true love sent to me
Twelve drummers drumming,
Eleven pipers piping,
Ten lords a-leaping,
Nine ladies dancing,
Eight maids a-milking,
Seven swans a-swimming,
Six geese a-laying,
Five golden rings,
Four calling birds,
Three French hens,
Two turtle doves,
And a partridge in a pear tree.

1

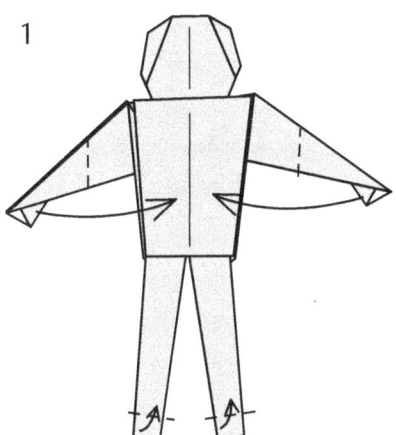

Begin with step 29 of the Lord a-Leaping (page 38). Make valley folds.

2

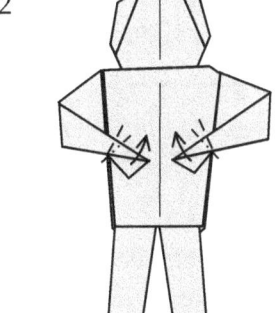

Pleat folds.

3

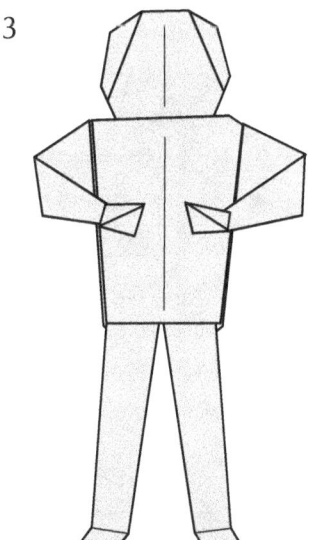

Drummer Drumming

Drummers Drumming 43

Drum

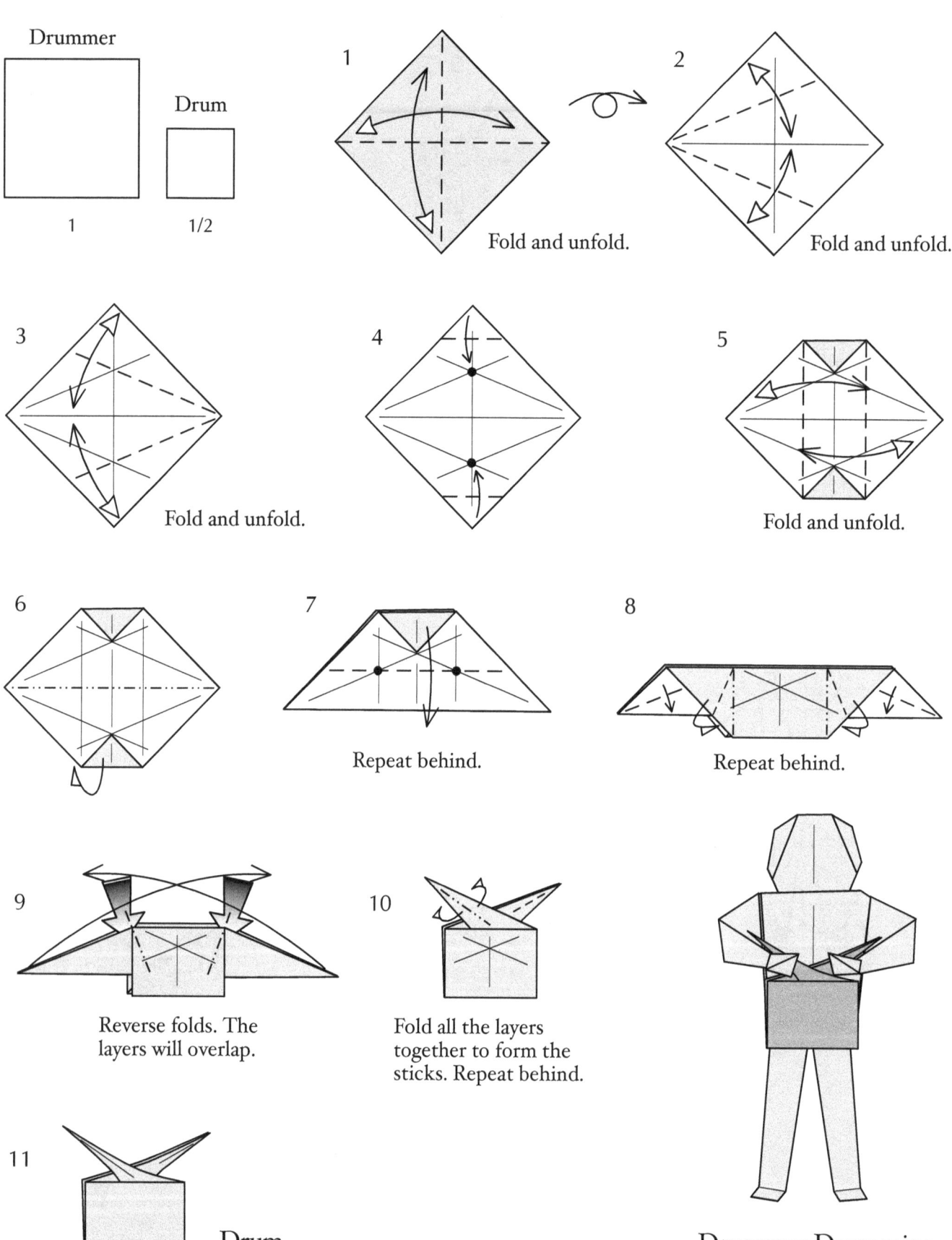

Drummer Drumming

44 *Origami Twelve Days of Christmas*

And Santa, too!

Fold Santa Claus, toys, boxes, and Chrismas tree ornaments.

Fancy Card

Traditional

1
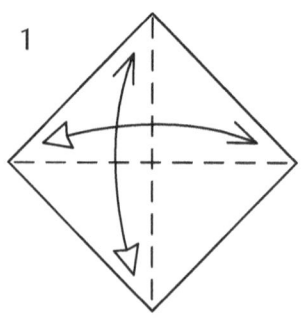
Fold and unfold.

2
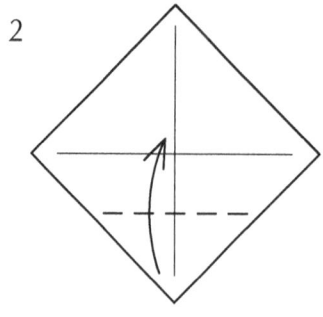
Fold above the center.

3
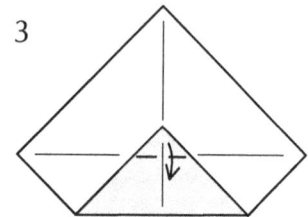
Fold along the hidden crease.

4
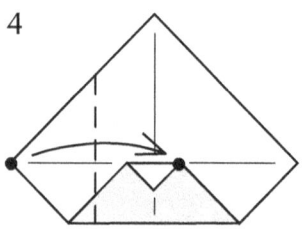
The dots will meet.

5
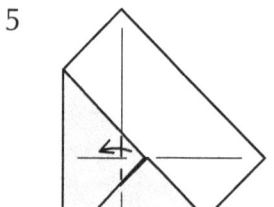
Fold along the hidden crease.

6
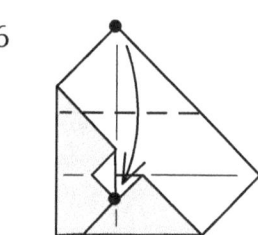
The dots will meet.

7
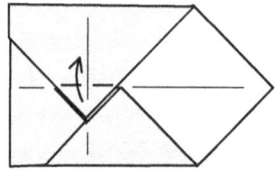
Fold along the hidden crease.

8
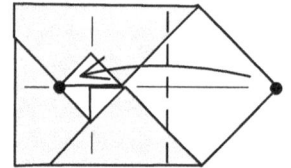
The dots will meet.

9
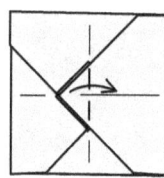
Fold along the hidden crease.

10
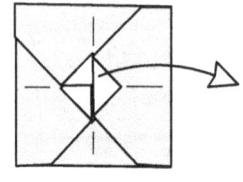
Unfold.

11
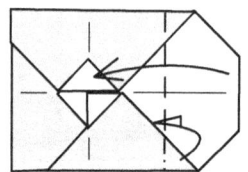
Reverse-fold.

12
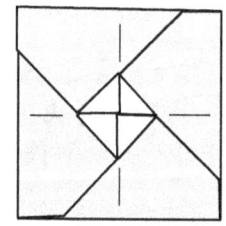
Fancy Card

Envelope

Traditional

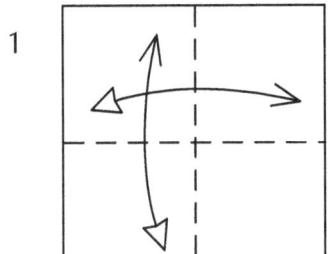
1. Fold and unfold.

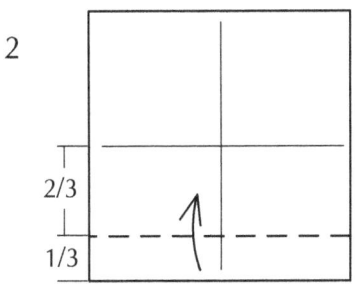
2. Fold up one-third.

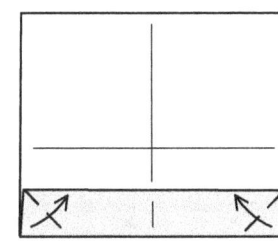
3.

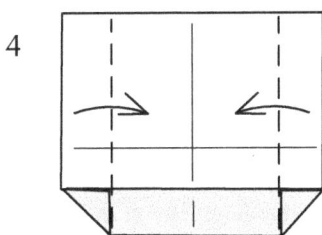
4.

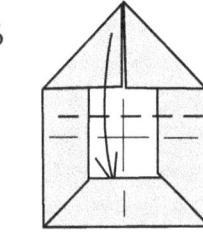
5. Fold to the center.

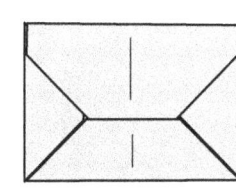
6. Tuck inside.

7. Envelope

Catamaran

Traditional

1. Fold and unfold.

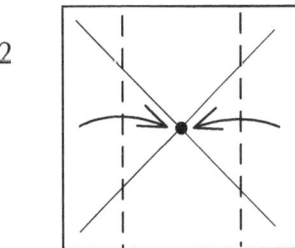
2. Fold to the center.

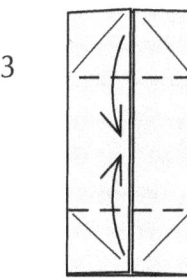
3. Fold to the center.

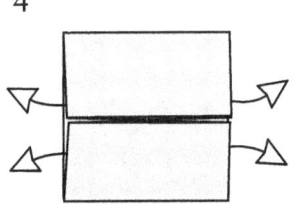
4. Pull out the corners.

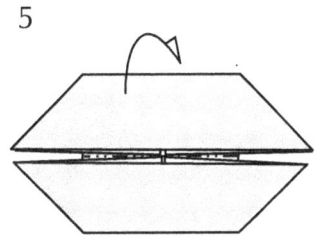
5. Fold behind.

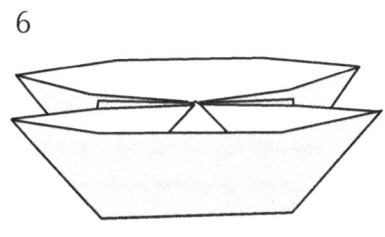
6. Catamaran

Envelope

Party Hat

Traditional

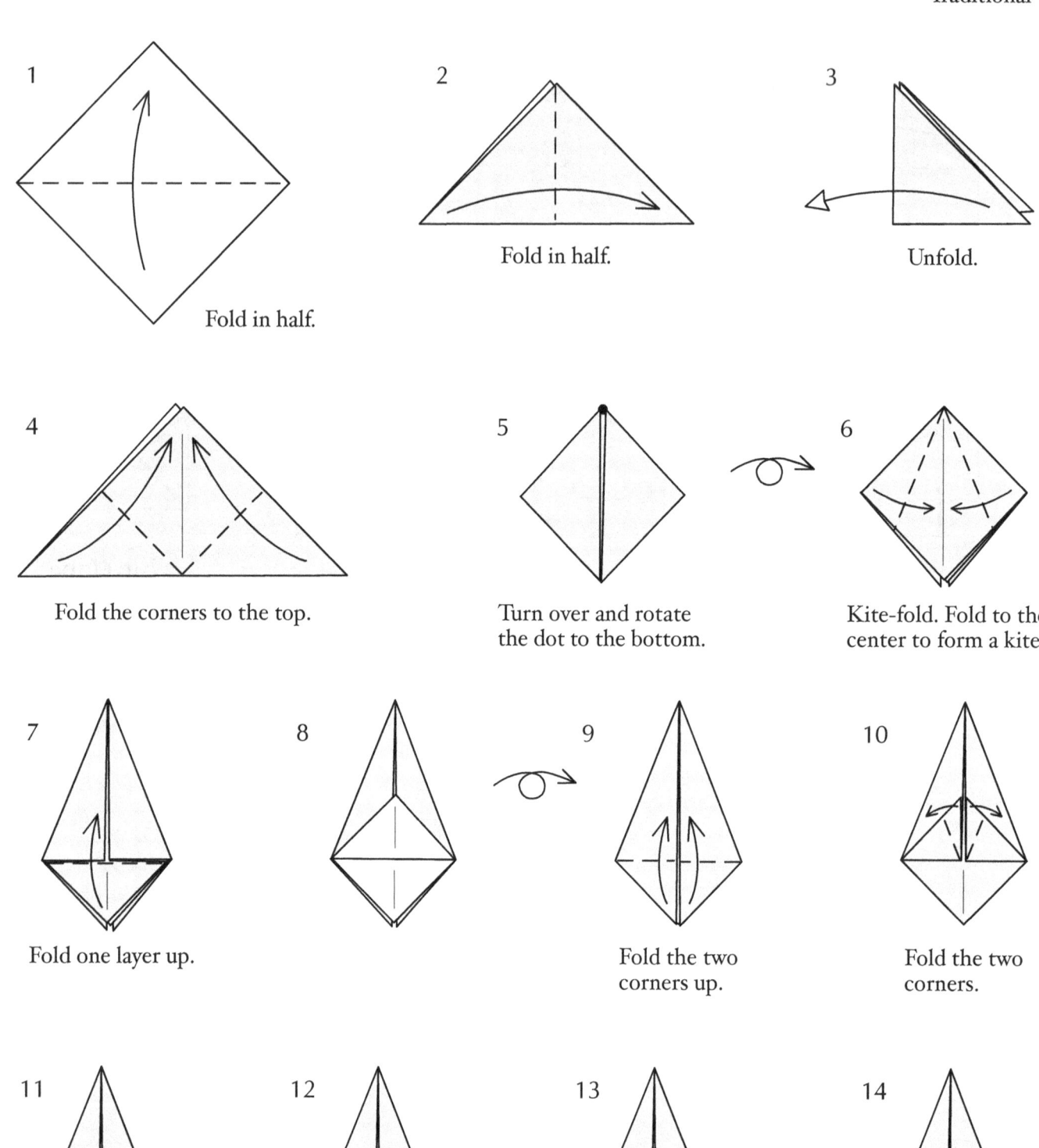

1. Fold in half.
2. Fold in half.
3. Unfold.
4. Fold the corners to the top.
5. Turn over and rotate the dot to the bottom.
6. Kite-fold. Fold to the center to form a kite.
7. Fold one layer up.
8.
9. Fold the two corners up.
10. Fold the two corners.
11. Fold up.
12. Fold a thin strip up.
13. Open the hat.
14. Party Hat

48 *Origami Twelve Days of Christmas*

Christmas Box

Traditional

1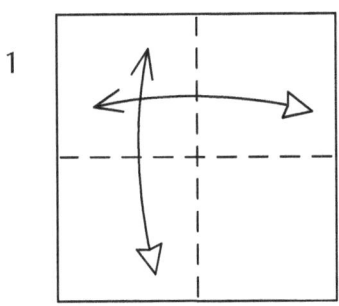
Fold and unfold.

2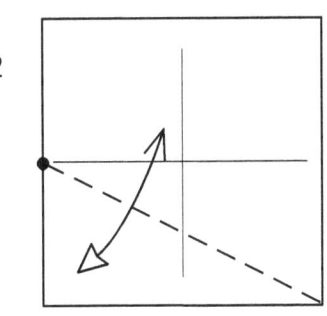
Fold and unfold.

3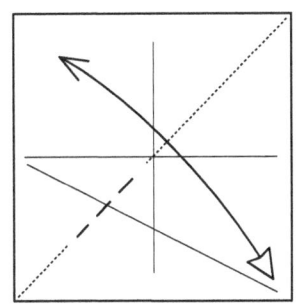
Fold and unfold creasing in the lower middle part.

4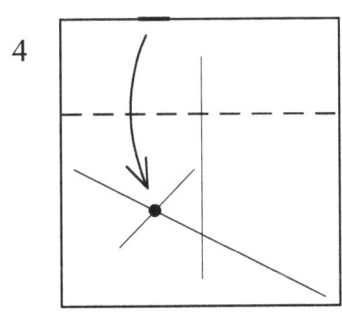
Bring the edge to the dot.

5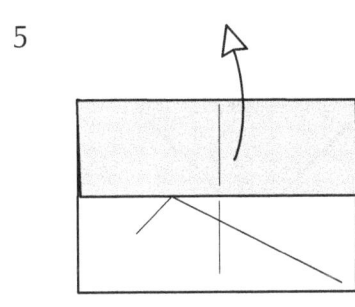
Unfold.

6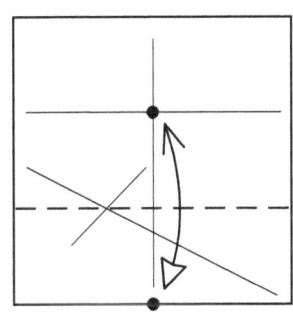
Fold and unfold.

7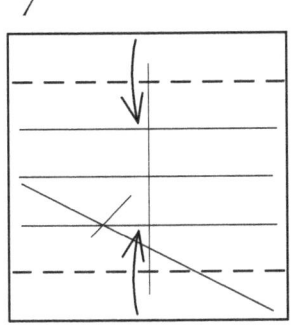

8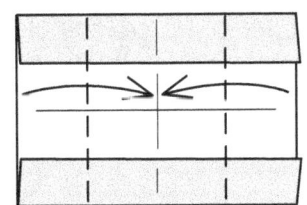

9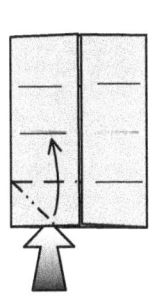
Squash-fold.

10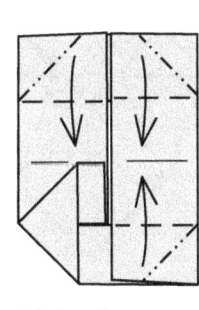
Make three more squash folds.

11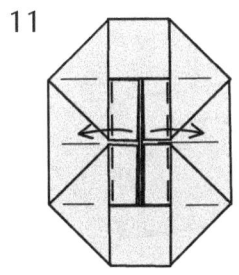

12
Open.

13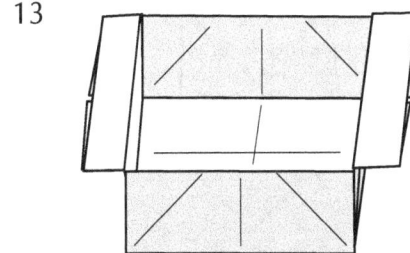
Christmas Box

Christmas Box 49

Gift Box

Traditional

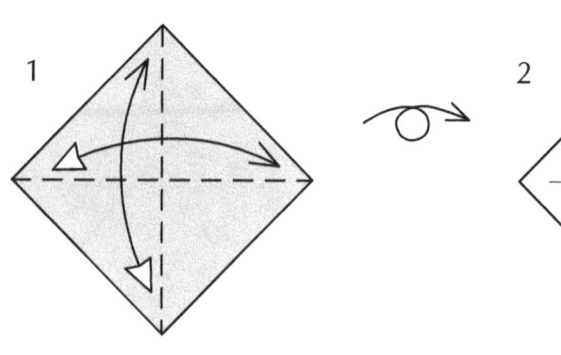

1. Fold and unfold.

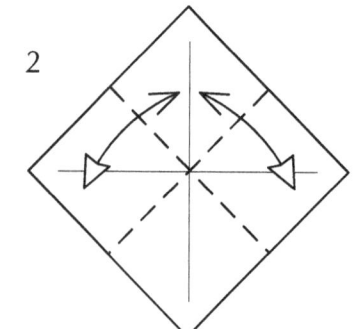

2. Fold and unfold.

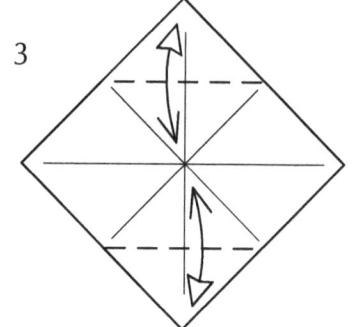

3. Fold and unfold opposite corners to the center.

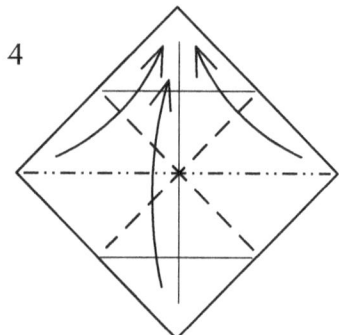

4. Refold along the creases.

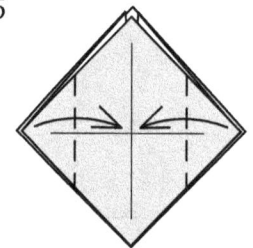

5. Fold to the center. Repeat behind.

6. Fold to the center. Repeat behind.

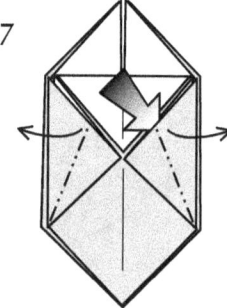

7. Squash folds. Repeat behind.

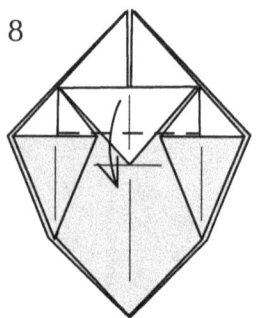

8. Fold down. Repeat behind.

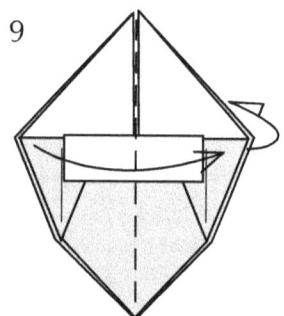

9. Fold the top left flap to the right and repeat behind.

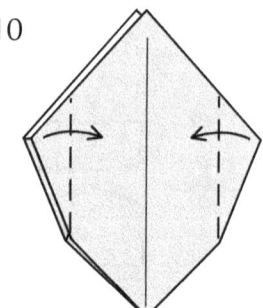

10. Fold towards the center. Repeat behind.

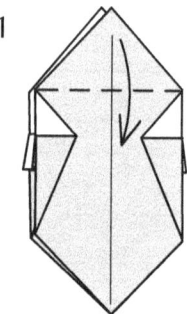

11. Fold down. Repeat behind.

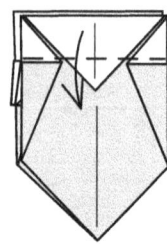

12. Fold down. Repeat behind.

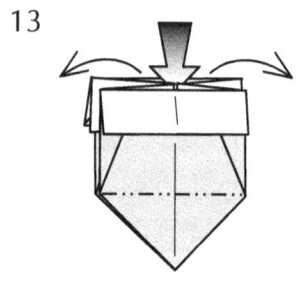

13. Open.

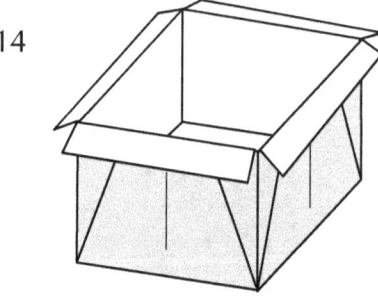

14. Gift Box

Origami Twelve Days of Christmas

Candy Dish

Traditional

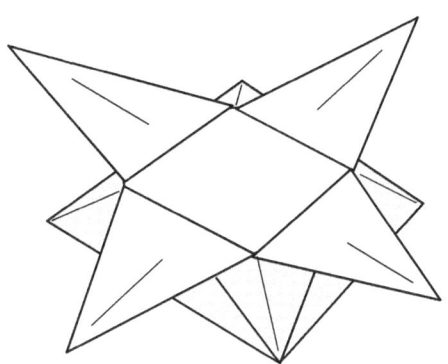

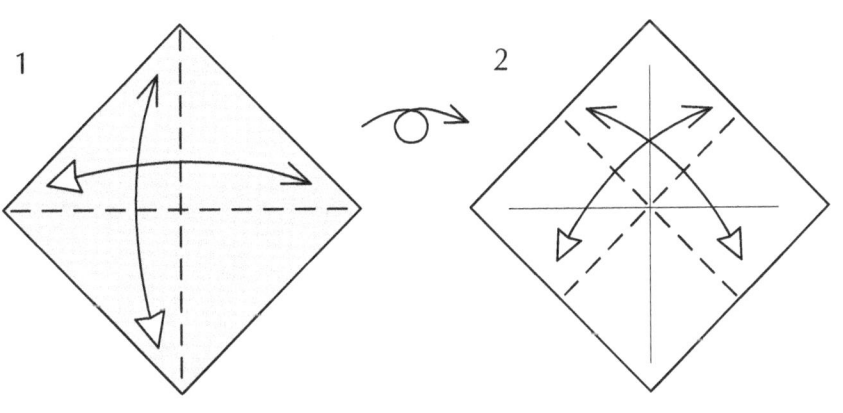

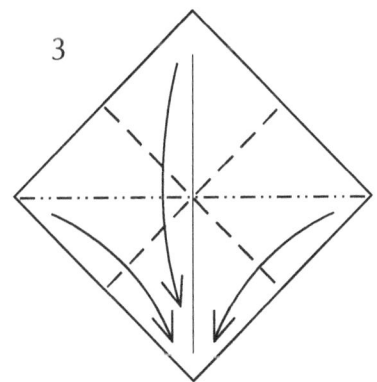

1. Fold and unfold.
2. Fold and unfold.
3. Fold along the creases.

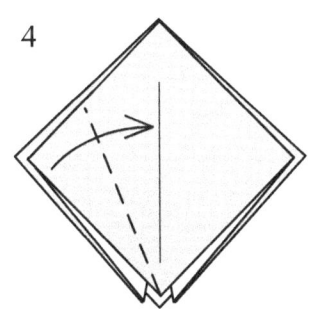

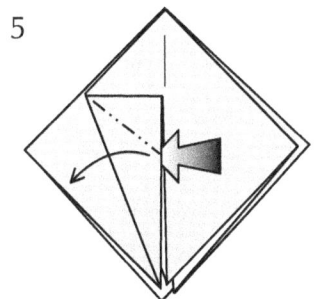

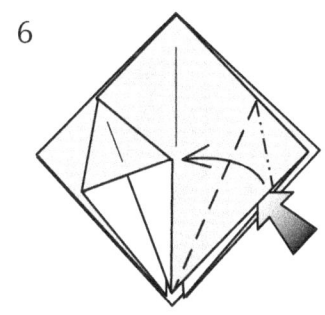

4. This is the Preliminary Fold.
5. Squash-fold.
6. Squash-fold.

Candy Dish 51

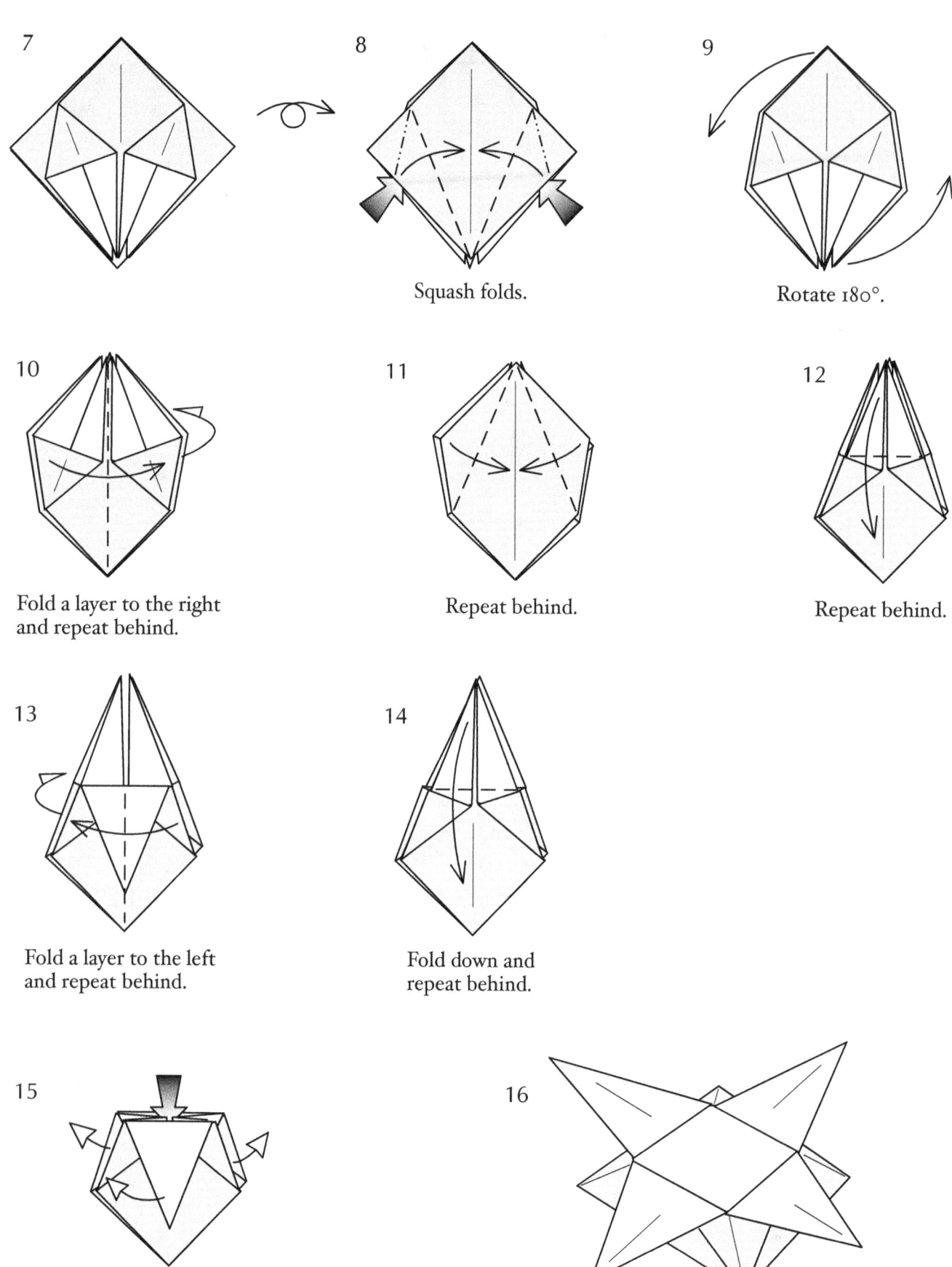

52 *Origami Twelve Days of Christmas*

Four-Pointed Star

Traditional

1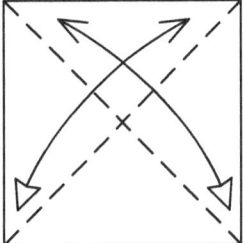
Fold and unfold.

2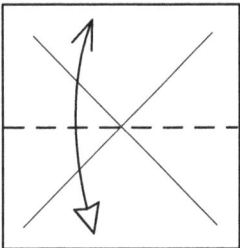
Fold and unfold.

3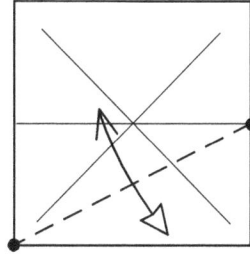
Fold and unfold.

4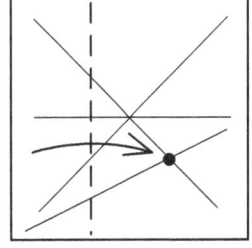
Fold to the dot.

5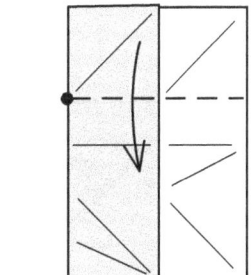

6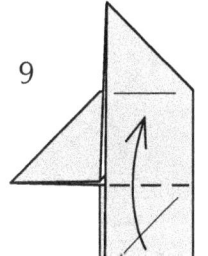
Pull out the corner.

7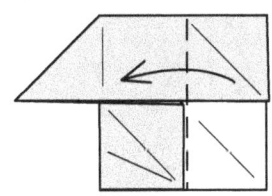

8
Pull out the corner.

9

10
Pull out the corner.

11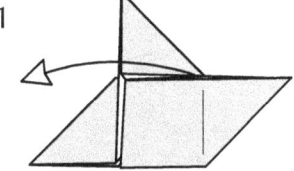
Pull out the corner.

12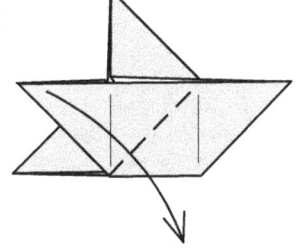

13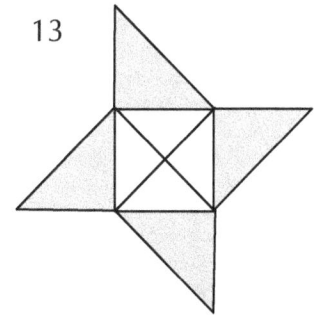
Four-Pointed Star

Five-Pointed Star

Traditional

1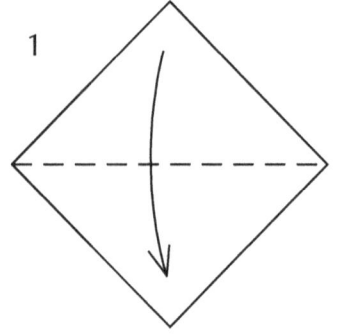
Fold in half.

2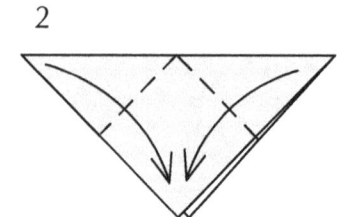

3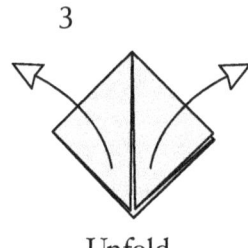
Unfold.

4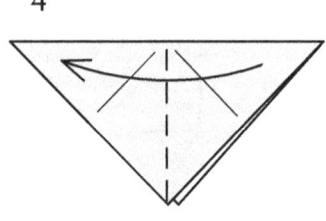
Fold in half.

5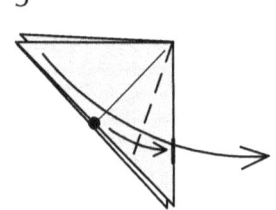
Fold the dot to the bold line.

6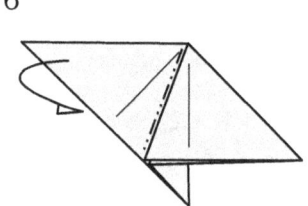
Fold behind.

7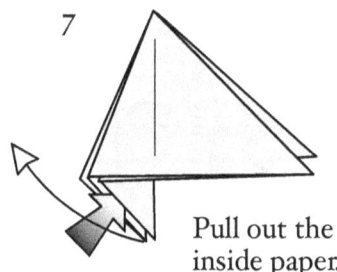
Pull out the inside paper.

8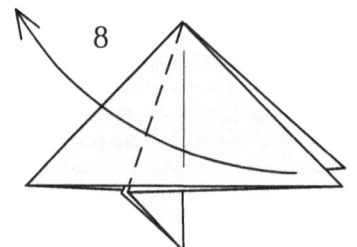

9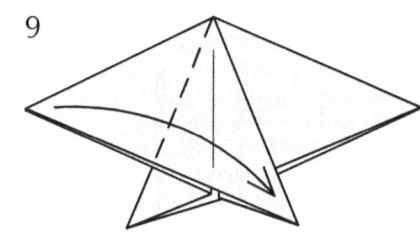

10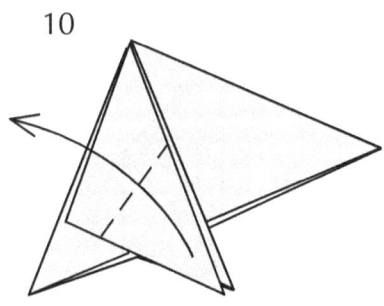
There are no guide lines for this fold.

11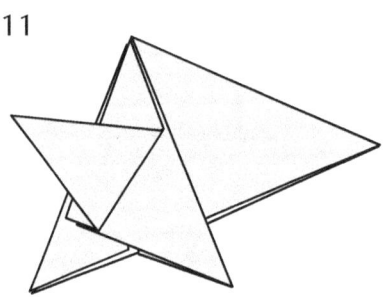
Repeat steps 9 and 10 behind.

12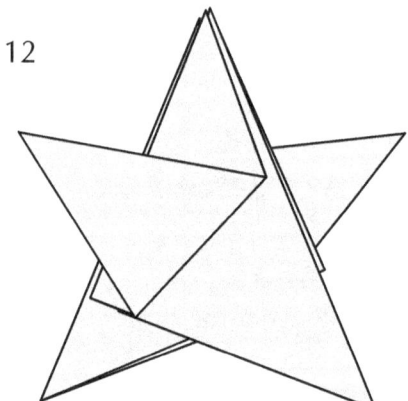
Five-Pointed Star

Candle

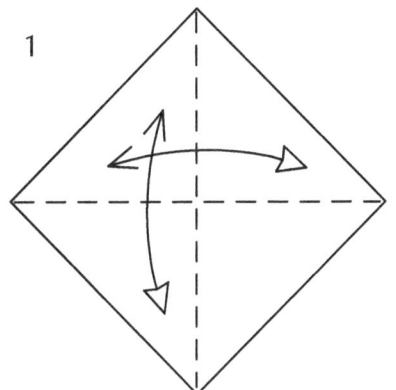

Fold and unfold.

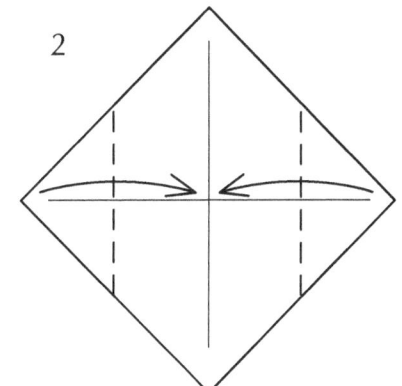

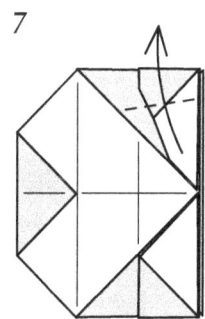

1. Fold to the center.
2. Fold and unfold.

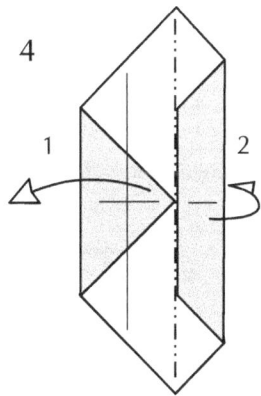

1. Unfold.
2. Fold behind.

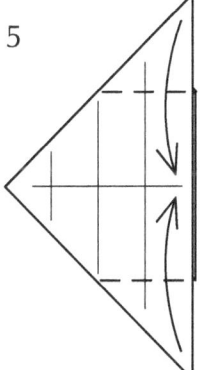

1. Fold behind.
2. Fold along the crease.

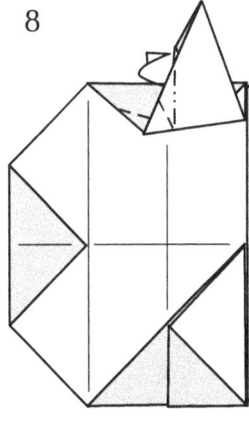

Fold inside.

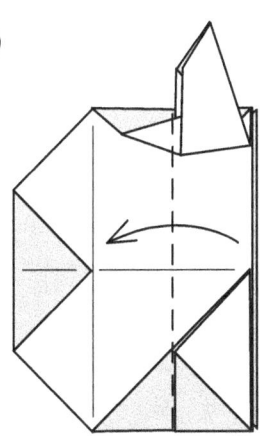

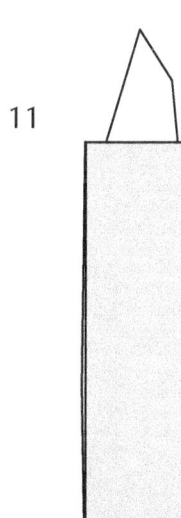

1. Tuck inside.
2. Make the bottom 3D.

Candle

Candle 55

Stocking

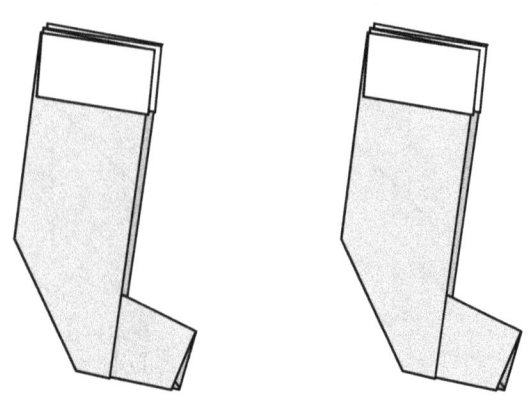

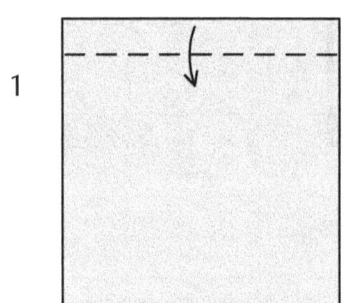

1 Fold a strip down. The size can vary.

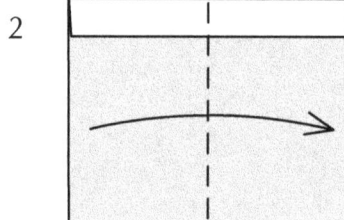

2

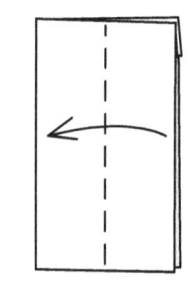

3 Repeat behind.

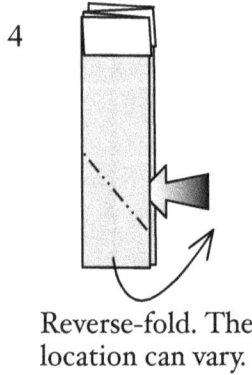

4 Reverse-fold. The location can vary.

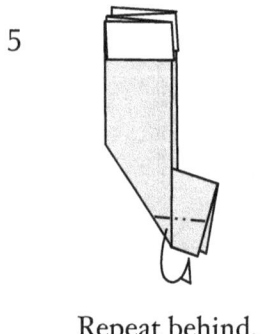

5 Repeat behind.

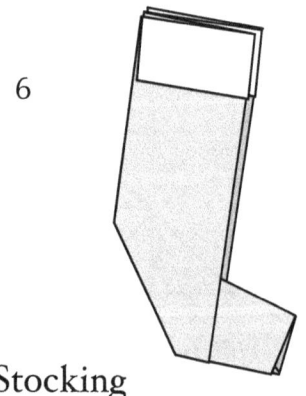

6 Stocking

56 *Origami Twelve Days of Christmas*

Bauble

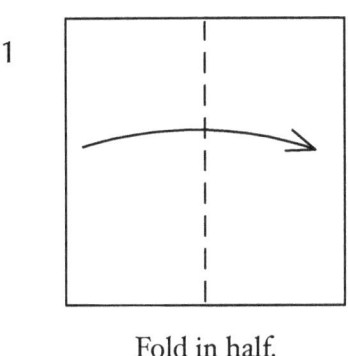
1. Fold in half.

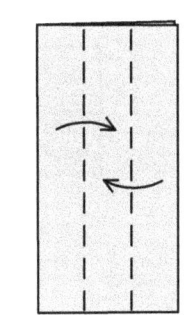
2. Fold in thirds.

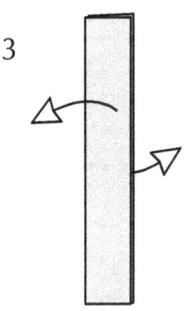
3. Unfold.

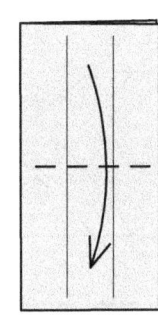
4. Fold in half.

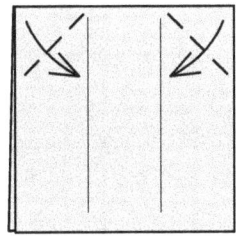
5. Fold to the creases.

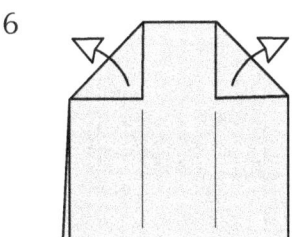
6. Unfold.

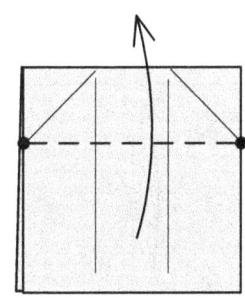
7. Fold the top layers.

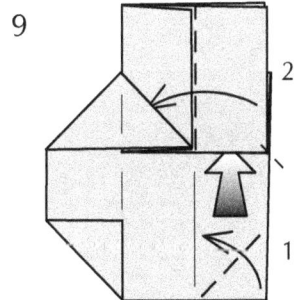
8.
1. Valley-fold.
2. Squash-fold.

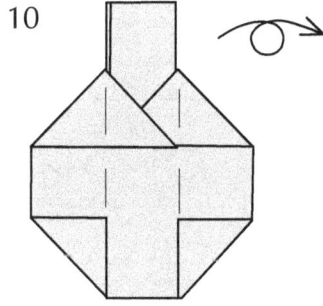
9.
1. Valley-fold.
2. Squash-fold and tuck inside.

10.

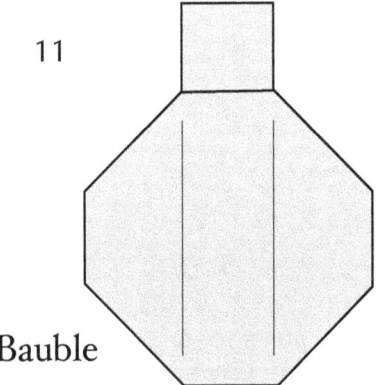
11. Bauble

Wreath

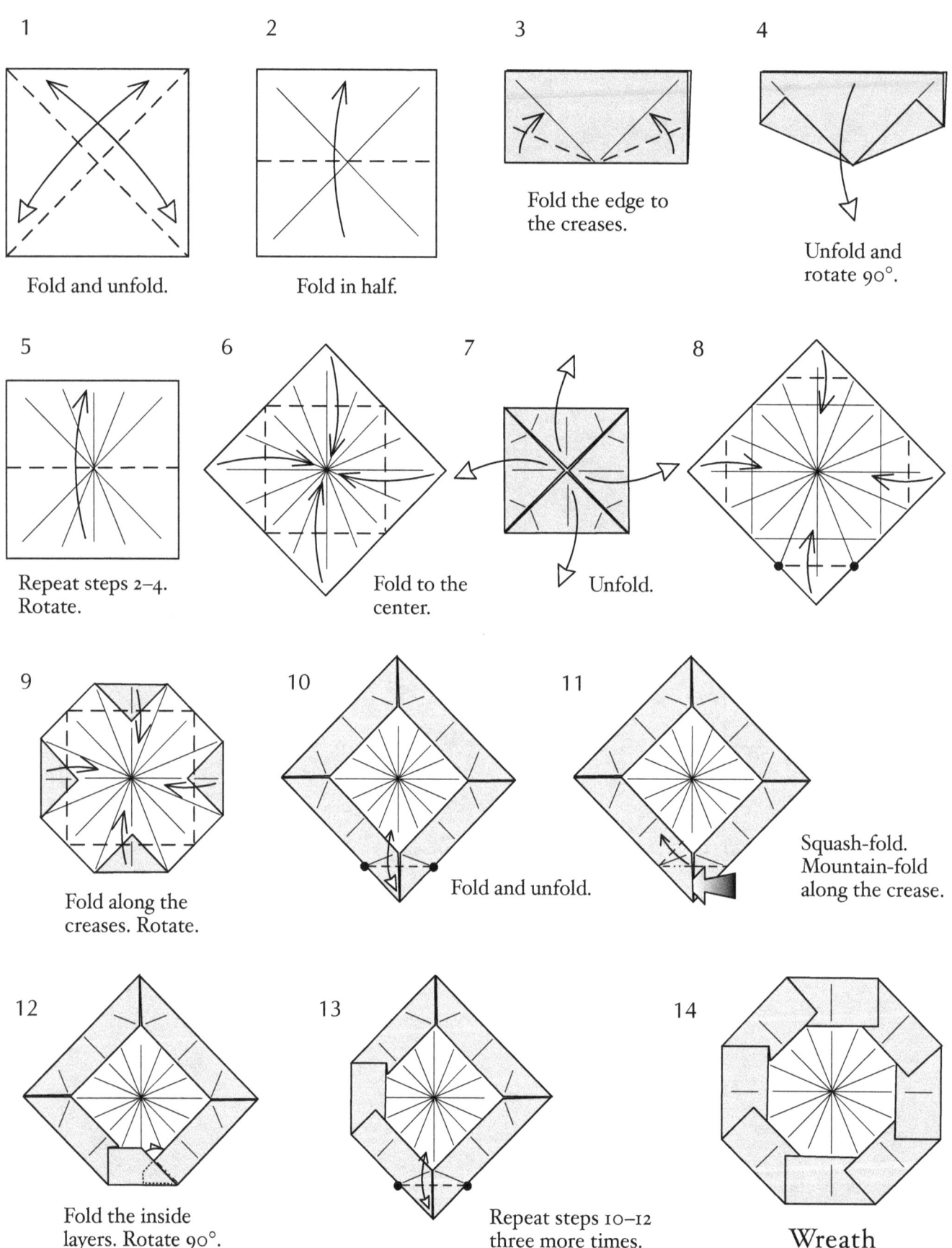

58   *Origami Twelve Days of Christmas*

Church

Traditional

1 Fold and unfold.

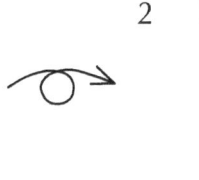 2 Fold and unfold.

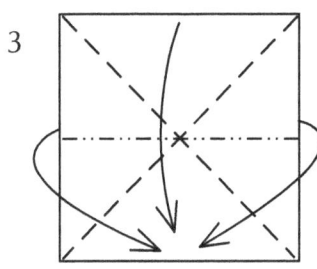 3 Collapse along the creases.

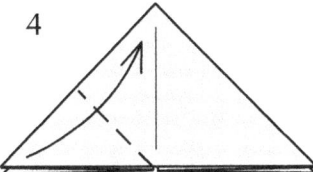 4 This is the Waterbomb Base. Fold the flap up.

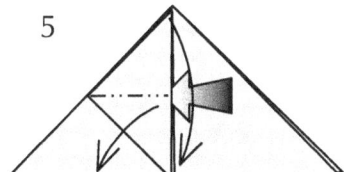 5 Squash-fold.

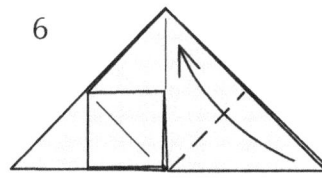 6 Repeat steps 4–5 on the right.

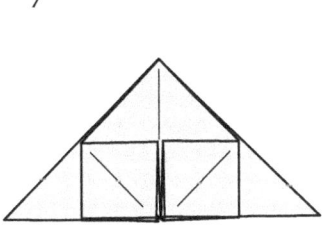 7 Repeat steps 4–6 behind.

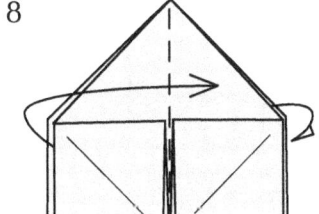 8 Fold to the right and repeat behind. This is a minor miracle.

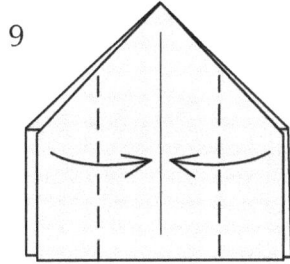 9 Fold the top layers to the center. Repeat behind.

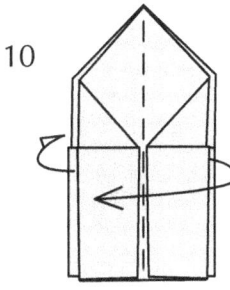 10 Minor miracle.

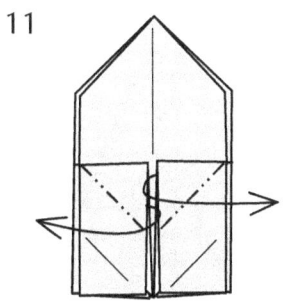 11 Squash folds.

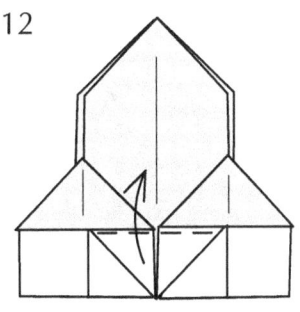 12 Fold up.

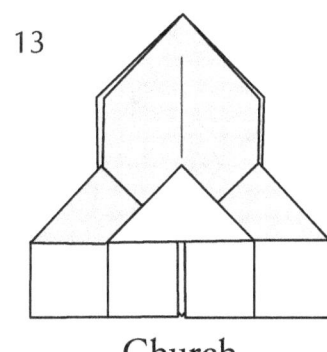 13 Church

Church 59

Simple Santa

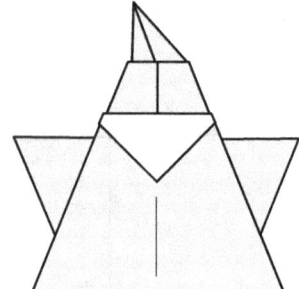

1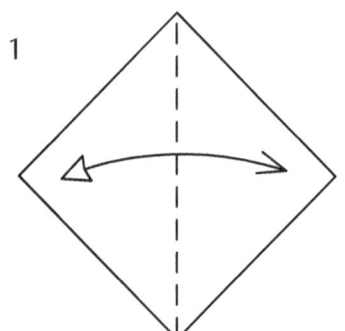
Fold and unfold.

2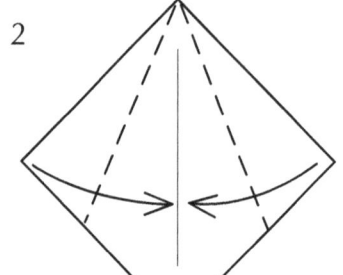
Fold to the center.

3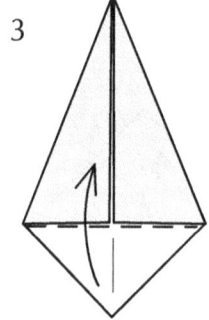
Fold up.

4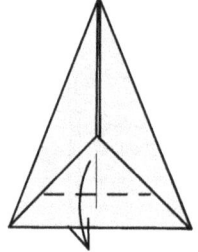
Fold down.

5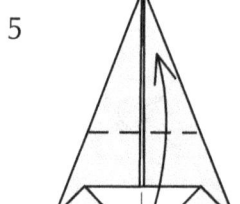
Fold up. The size can vary.

6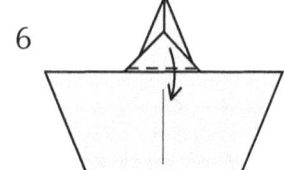
Fold down.

7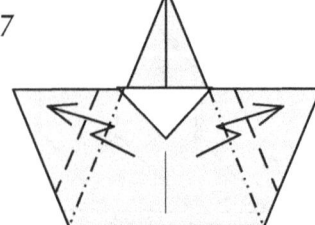
Fold back and forth.

8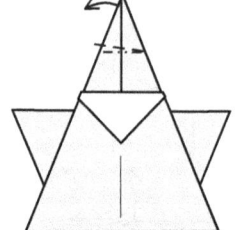
Fold back and forth.

9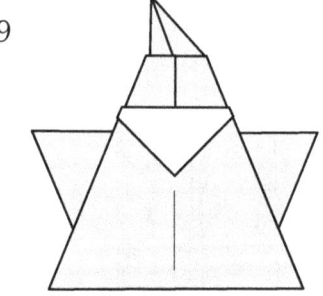
Santa

60 *Origami Twelve Days of Christmas*

Santa Claus

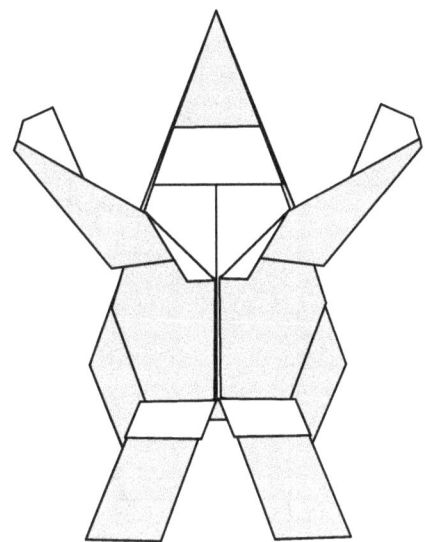

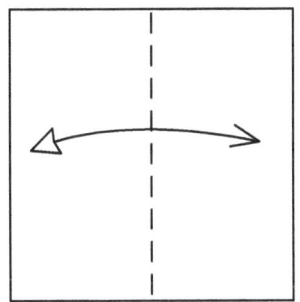

1

Fold and unfold.

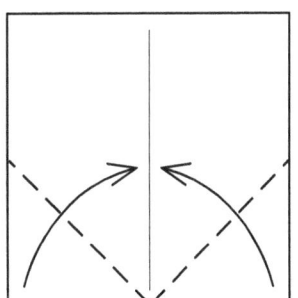

2

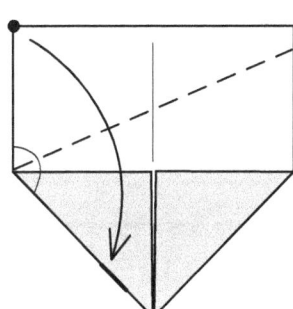

3

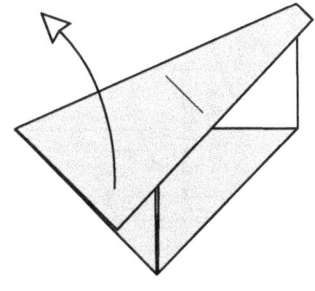

4

Unfold.

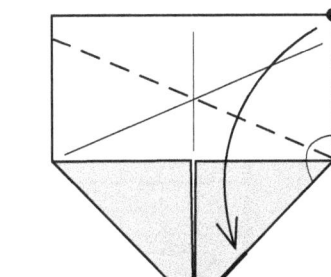

5

Repeat steps 3–4 in the opposite direction.

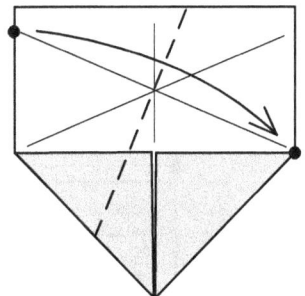

6

Santa Claus 61

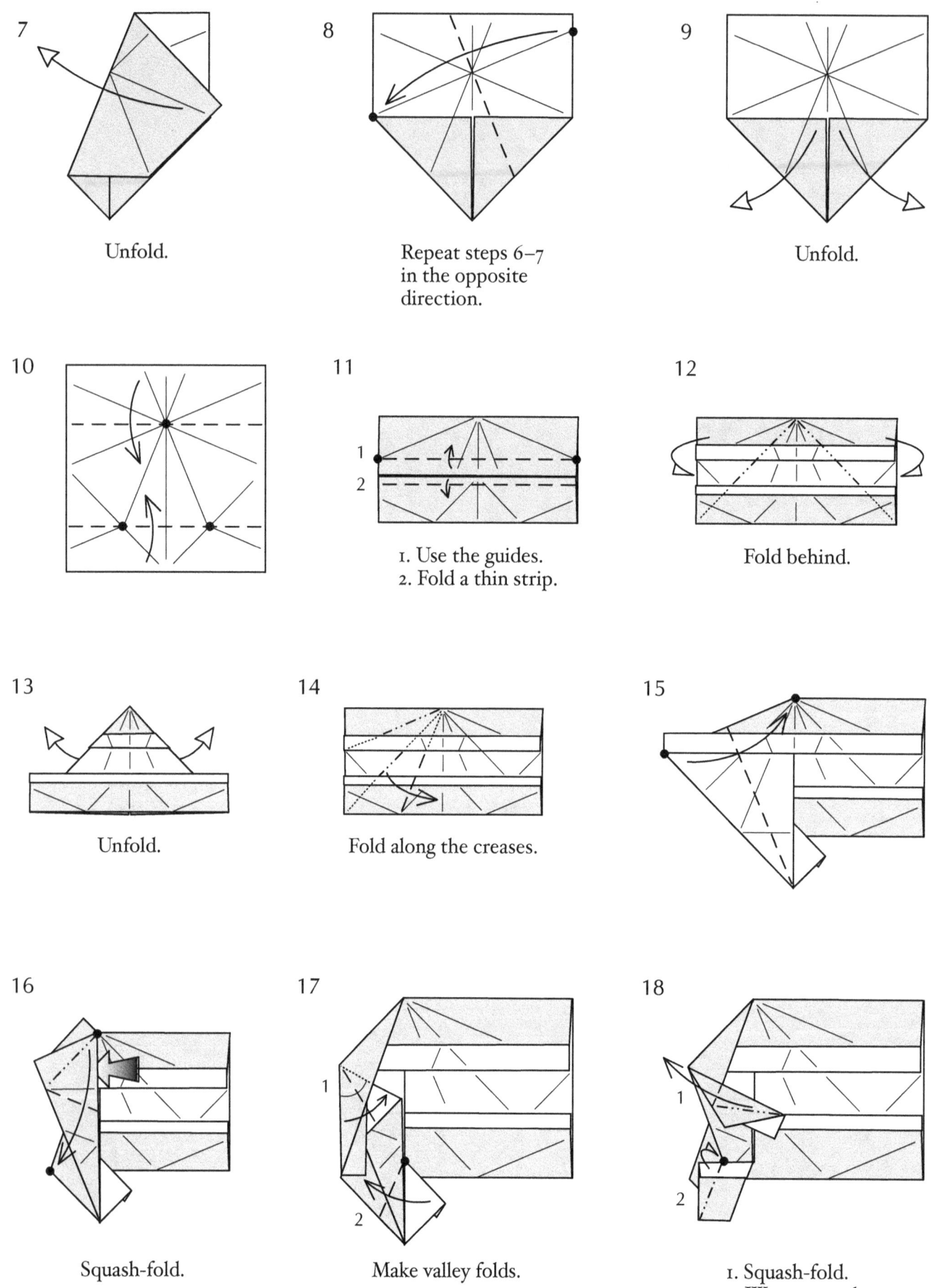

19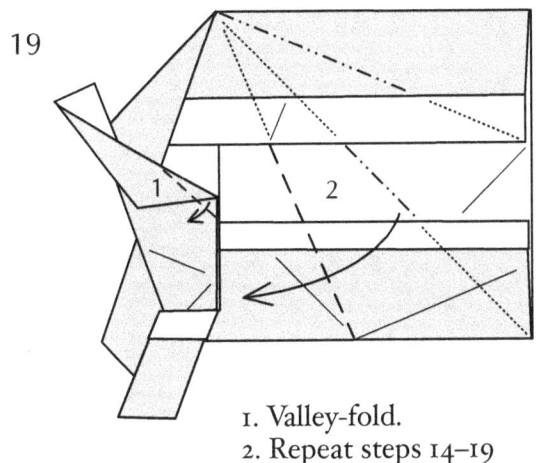

1. Valley-fold.
2. Repeat steps 14–19 on the right.

20

21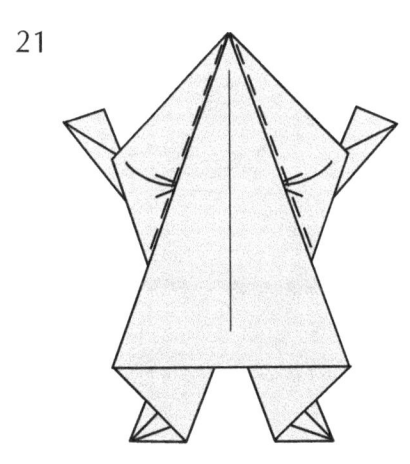

Tuck inside.

22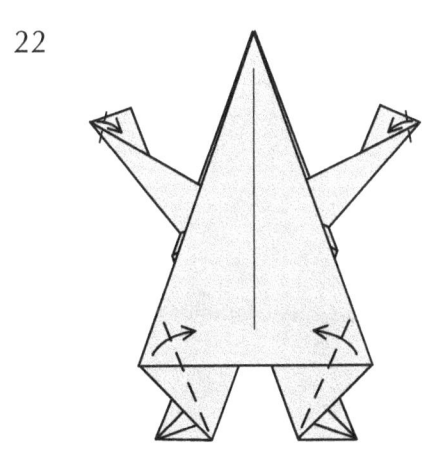

23

24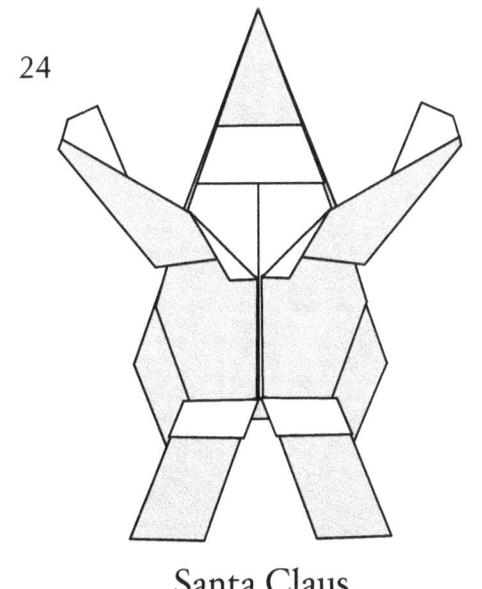

Santa Claus

www.ingramcontent.com/pod-product-compliance
Lightning Source LLC
Chambersburg PA
CBHW081127080526
44587CB00021B/3775